THE
····

DISRUPTION MINDSET

Dana: All the best
thing with disruption!

Also by Charlene Li

The Engaged Leader

The Seven Success Factors of Social Business Strategy,
co-authored with Brian Solis

Open Leadership

Marketing in the Groundswell, co-authored with Josh Bernoff

Groundswell, co-authored with Josh Bernoff

THE DISRUPTION MINDSET

Why Some
Organizations
Transform While
Others Fail

Charlene Li

New York Times Bestselling
Author of *Open Leadership*

IDEAPRESS
PUBLISHING

Published in the United States by Ideapress Publishing.

IDEAPRESS PUBLISHING | WWW.IDEAPRESSPUBLISHING.COM

All trademarks are the property of their respective companies.

Cataloging-in-Publication Data is on file with the Library of Congress.
ISBN: 978-1940858708

PROUDLY PRINTED IN THE UNITED STATES OF AMERICA
BY SELBY MARKETING ASSOCIATES

SPECIAL SALES

Ideapress Books are available at a special discount for bulk purchases for sales promotions and premiums, or for use in corporate training programs. Special editions, including personalized covers, a custom foreword, corporate imprints and bonus content are also available.

No animals were harmed in the writing, printing or distribution of this book. The trees, unfortunately, were not so lucky.

Dedicated with the deepest gratitude to my partner in life and love, Côme Laguë. Your unwavering support gave me the confidence and strength to live out of my comfort zone every day.

CONTENTS

THE
DISRUPTION MINDSET

"Growth is painful.
Change is painful.
But, nothing is
as painful as staying
stuck where you
do not belong."

—N. R. Narayana Murthy, co-founder of Infosys

INTRODUCTION
· · · · · · · · · · · · · · · · · ·

———————————●———————————

A
S AN author, analyst, and entrepreneur in the technology space, I've had the opportunity to watch and work with many organizations as they try to become disruptive but eventually fail.

I personally experienced this kind of failure early in my career. When I graduated from Harvard Business School in 1993, I saw the Internet revolution coming and wanted to be in the middle of it. I took a job at the *San Jose Mercury News*, a newspaper in the heart of Silicon Valley. That year, it had launched Mercury Center, an electronic version of the newspaper, on AOL, and by late 1994, it was one of the first newspapers to have an online presence. I helped create our digital advertising offerings and trained the unionized sales force on how to sell banner ads.

Mercury News was part of Knight Ridder, at the time one of the largest newspaper publishers in the United States. It set up a separate organization—Knight Ridder Digital—to address the emerging needs of the online audience and capitalize on emerging digital opportunities.[1] One of Knight Ridder Digital's first major projects was the Real Cities Network, a set of city guides on the Web affiliated with the company's newspapers and designed to digitally dominate the content and advertising in each of their cities.

Despite a promising start and substantial investment in this separate unit, the company couldn't gain significant traction in the digital space.

Meanwhile, revenues and profits from its print operations continued to drop. In 2006, Knight Ridder was sold at auction to McClatchy Newspapers.[2] What was once the nation's second-largest newspaper chain ceased to exist.

A hemisphere away, a different story was unfolding at Schibsted, the largest newspaper group in Norway.[3] Like Knight Ridder, it also anticipated the coming digital disruption and in 1995 committed to following readers and advertisers to whatever channel they chose. It bought an Internet service provider that included a search engine (similar to AltaVista) and a website catalog (similar to Yahoo!). In 1999 it started what would eventually become Finn.no, an online classifieds site, and in 2003 Schibsted bought Blocket, the leading Swedish online player. Seeing an opportunity, the company replicated the Finn.no and Blocket models, rolling out the online classified sites in other countries.

Its strategy paid off: the cash from those sites helped fuel a global expansion of media operations. In 2018, Schibsted's marketplace sites were the leading online marketplaces in twenty-three countries, including France, Spain, Sweden, and Brazil, and represented 47 percent of Schibsted's revenues and 90 percent of its gross operating profit.[4] Its flagship newspapers in Norway and Sweden continue to replace declining print revenues with online advertising and digital subscriptions while increasing their operating margin.

How did a newspaper company in Norway manage to become a digital disruptor and thrive while Knight Ridder failed, despite being in the middle of Silicon Valley and following prescribed strategies from the leading strategists of the day?

Simple. Knight Ridder approached disruption from the wrong end.

WE'VE BEEN APPROACHING DISRUPTION BACKWARD

Like Knight Ridder, many other established companies make disruption their goal and hope that growth will follow. They believe that their innovation will disrupt their market and drive growth. But that's not how it works: disruption doesn't create growth; growth creates disruption.

Most innovation efforts fail because they focus on developing innovations without thinking through whether, and how, these will create growth and change. The independent innovation centers or groups designed to lead these efforts are rarely in a position to make the tough choices that truly lead to disruptive transformation: How will we bet our company's future on the next-generation customer instead of today's steady and reliable one? How do we abandon our current business model for an entirely new one? They also don't have to deal with the very messy reactions people have to these decisions—or the massive cultural transformation that they often demand.

Growth is always hard. Breakthrough growth is even harder. It is disruptive precisely because it shifts the balance of power in established relationships—between customers and companies, between players in an industry, between people and departments within an organization. Growth challenges our attachment to proven revenue streams and customers while nurturing our ambitions to discover new ones.

For example, disruptive e-commerce innovations alter the relationship between organizations and their customers, giving people more choice and power to shift their buying to new entrants like Etsy and eyeglass retailer Warby Parker. Disruptive business models change the business ecosystems by transferring power from traditional industry players like the taxi industry to new platforms like Uber and Go-Jek in Indonesia. Disruptive communication tools, like social collaboration and videoconferencing platforms such as Slack and Skype, shift relationships within organizations as frontline employees can now speak to and hear from top executives directly via digital channels without the intervention of middle managers.

These power shifts are deeply unsettling—not just from a business model standpoint but also from a psychological one. That's where the "disruption" comes from: our safe, familiar world is turned upside down. *Disruptive transformation is so difficult because it upsets the status quo and shifts power relationships.* It requires not settling for the table that is set for us and instead committing to run toward a future that is radically different from and better than where we are today.

Knight Ridder failed because it didn't anticipate and address the distress that rose from these power shifts within the organization. It created a separate unit to "disrupt" the online news space but had no meaningful strategy for how those innovations would drive growth across the rest of the company. It essentially quarantined fear and disruption. The powerful local newspaper publishers were used to running their domains independently. But without a clear vision for how these digital innovations would grow enlarge their slice of the pie in the future, they bristled at having to support a corporate digital initiative that distracted their editorial and ad sales staff away from what was a lucrative print business at the time. In the end, Knight Ridder couldn't get past warring publishers. The best innovations in the world wouldn't have saved it.

Helping you avoid the fate of Knight Ridder, Blockbuster, Sears, and dozens of others is what *The Disruption Mindset* is all about. It's about helping you move from talking wistfully and vaguely about "disruption" to making disruptive transformation and exponential growth—and embracing the messy, emotional power dynamics that come with it—a part of your agenda every day.

WHAT IS DISRUPTIVE TRANSFORMATION?

The word *disruption* has been misused and appropriated over the past couple of decades. Before we can talk about what disruptive transformation *is* and how to harness it, let's get a few things straight about what disruptive transformation *isn't*.

It's not only innovation. Innovation is easy. Disruption is hard. Many companies want innovation to be a carefully managed process with minimal disruption to the status quo. I once served on an "innovation committee" where one of the criteria was a six-month return on investments, which guaranteed that any approved initiative would have minimal impact. Innovation is the snooze button of corporate strategy, pushing tough decisions into the future. Don't settle for innovation alone.

It's not about technology. I'm frequently asked to speak about the disruptive innovation that will disrupt the fill-in-the-blank industry. I point out to these clients that it's rarely a new technology that creates disruption. Instead, it's the application of existing technologies in new ways that enables disruption. Uber, for example, was a simple app that matched available drivers with riders, transforming the customer experience using GPS tracking and seamless account payment. While each of these technologies had existed for years, it was bundling them together that was unique and disruptive.

It's not always fast and unpredictable. Disruption is a slow process.[5] Napster debuted in 2000 when the global recorded music industry had $23.4 billion in revenue. Two years later, the industry had declined, but only to $21.9 billion.[6] Napster forever changed how we share and listen to music, but it, and the change it ushered in, didn't hurt the music industry overnight. The problem is that the response from challenged incumbents is even slower. They squander their few years of grace when they can instead do something about the impending disruption.

It isn't only for start-ups. The classic description of a disruptive company is of a start-up challenging established incumbents. However, arguably the most disruptive companies on the planet today are also the largest ones: Amazon, Apple, Facebook, and Google. Like them, incumbents' organizations have the customer relationships, scale, and cash to create massive disruptions—but only if they can get out of their way

So what *is* disruptive transformation? I define *transformation* as "the process of changing from one state to another." You can go through that change process in a gradual, incremental way that causes as little discomfort as possible. Or you can tackle it head-on and bear the stress and strain of the change to capture the opportunities created faster and sooner. In this book, I'm focusing on the latter because there is too much at stake, and too many problems and issues to address, to settle for the slow path. And frankly, if you go at a pace dictated by your comfort zone, you'll get left behind by your customers and the marketplace.

If disruptive transformation is the *process* you go through, the outcome at the other end is what makes it worth the journey: exponential growth. Let me be clear that I define *growth* broadly. While businesses measure growth as revenue and profits, a school would measure it differently, perhaps in terms of increasing opportunity and options for its students. A nonprofit would define growth as achieving its mission better and faster, and a religious organization may look at growth in a spiritual context.

"Disruption" has been reduced to the oversimplified myths I listed above because, in reality, it is far from straightforward. Disruptive transformation is complicated and elusive. It is more than just the right mix of product, timing, and strategy. It requires transforming the entire organization and its culture, and that starts with the mindset and behaviors of the leadership team.

THE THREE ELEMENTS OF DISRUPTIVE TRANSFORMATION

Over the years, I have seen a few organizations beat the odds and succeed at becoming disruptive. Their journeys all have one common thread: rather than shrink away from the daunting task of transforming themselves, disruptive transformation permeates every aspect of the organization and is on the agenda every single day. Disruption doesn't take days off.

My research uncovered three elements common to the organizations that have thrived with disruption and that I feature in this book. These elements not only informed which tactical moves each organization made to become disruptive but also helped them manage the very human emotional or psychological issues that rose from executing their strategy. With so many unknowns and uncertainties facing these incumbents, the three elements provided a foundation for their growth strategies. Here's a quick overview of each element.

Element #1: A Strategy Inspired by Future Customers to Make Big Gulp Decisions

To create disruptive transformation, you need a strategy—a plan of what you will do and won't do to achieve your objective because you can do anything but you can't do everything. The legendary ice hockey player Wayne Gretzky once said, "I skate to where the puck is going to be, not to where it has been." A disruptive transformation strategy requires that you turn your back on where the puck is today—your current customer, its attractive size and profitability—and anticipate where it is going to be in the future, where the growth and value potential will be. Customers will always move faster than the organizations chasing after them.

The implications for the organization are enormous and change everything. What most companies lack aren't strategic ideas but the ability to overcome departmental self-interests to fight for something worthy of the very tough journey ahead. Organizations fail to disrupt because they fall short of fully committing to a strategy centered on serving future customers; they cut corners rather than take on the full brunt of the angst and pain that this strategy will cause.

In contrast, disruptive organizations focus relentlessly on the needs of future customers to drive their growth, lifting the strategy above departmental battles or technology disagreements. The organizations featured in this book spent time and resources researching and understanding the unmet, unexpressed needs of people they would serve in the future. They built models of these nonexistent, next-generation customers and created a vision of how they would serve them. And they made sure that the organization and its strategy were aligned around that vision.

One example of this is T-Mobile. It could have followed the existing playbook of selling against network coverage and pricing promotions. Instead, it focused on the unexpressed, unaddressed frustrations of mobile customers with their "The Un-Carrier" strategy, which resulted in a doubling of revenues over five years to $40 billion and changing the economics for competitors AT&T and Verizon. The Un-Carrier strategy—with its centerpiece of getting rid of what was then the standard two-year contract—was far more than a branding campaign. T-Mobile had to change everything from the way it answered phones to way it gave incentives to salespeople.

Another example is Adobe. In 2011 the software giant could see that the revenue increases for its flagship Adobe Creative Suite software were coming primarily from price increases, not customer growth. Its leaders made the uncomfortable decision to abandon expensive, perpetual license software for a lower-priced, cloud-based subscription service to attract new customers. They knew changing their business model in such a way would trigger a significant, but temporary, decline in revenues and profits for twenty-four to thirty-six months—a potentially deadly blow for a publicly traded company. They also knew everything in the business would need to change, from how they developed products to how they provided customer support.

But their bet paid off. In 2012, Adobe's revenue was $4.4 billion and net earnings were $833 million. By 2018 revenue had risen to $9 billion and net earnings to $2.8 billion, more than a two-times increase in revenue and three-times increase in net earnings over seven years. Moreover, its stock price had risen seven times. What allowed Adobe to make this bold—and disruptive—move was a laser-like focus on meeting the needs of future customers.

As you'll see in the book, organizations like T-Mobile and Adobe become disruptive by aligning with the fastest-moving part of their ecosystem to create a vision and purpose—a "why" that everyone in the organization can understand and, more important, believe in: growth. Growth is the magic elixir that soothes the disrupted soul of the organization, acting as the shock absorbers on the rough journey.

In Chapter 1, I'll delve more deeply into T-Mobile's story and show how to set your strategy based on your future customers—from how to identify them to how to align your strategy around them. In Chapter 2, I'll explain how Adobe prepared itself to make the highly contentious and difficult "big gulp" decisions that are at the center of disruptive transformation strategies—and how you and your organization can too.

Element #2: Leadership That Creates a Movement of Disruptors

Creating and sustaining breakthrough growth is soul-sucking work, but someone has to do it. Leaders create change and nurture environments where change can flourish.[7] But disruptive change, because of the enormity of the transformation it entails, requires a special kind of leadership. It requires that leaders actively and systematically create a movement to achieve the future desired state.

If the vision of the desired future state is the flint, a movement is the fuel that keeps the fire burning. There will be times when the road ahead is strewn with boulders and being part of a movement sustains and energizes people to find a way to climb over those obstacles.

When you are part of something bigger than yourself, you set aside your personal pain and discomfort to achieve that shared goal.

Consider, for example, Dr. Martin Luther King Jr. and the other civil rights leaders in the 1960s. When Dr. King delivered his famous "I Have a Dream" speech, he painted in vivid strokes what was at that time an unimaginable future. He knew the daunting challenges facing the people assembled on the Washington Mall in August 1963 and that the civil rights movement would need to be energized for years to come. But he didn't stop there. When Dr. King stepped off the podium, he and the other civil rights movement leaders excelled at organizing, structuring, and empowering thousands of other leaders to take action in their communities.

Like Dr. King, the disruptive leaders interviewed for this book exhibited two characteristics that are needed to create a movement. First, they develop what I call an "openness-to-change mindset," that is, they are comfortable with uncertainty and unafraid to try new things. The second is that they develop leadership behaviors that empower and inspire followers—they build a coalition of key people to make change happen and empower them to try new approaches to their work.

To learn more about these disruptive leadership mindsets and behaviors, I surveyed 1,087 leaders in the United States, United Kingdom, Germany, China, and Brazil. I asked them to assess how much disruptive change they believe they are capable of leading and to rate themselves on some of the key mindsets and behaviors necessary to lead disruption. My findings revealed that being disruptive is not an absolute: leaders' desire to change the status quo varies greatly. To outline the various ways that disruptiveness manifests itself, I developed four archetypes of disruptive leaders: Steadfast Managers, Realist Optimists, Worried Skeptics, and Agent Provocateur.

In Chapter 3, I describe in greater detail how to create a movement—from writing your manifesto for change to leading a movement in the digital age—and show how two very different leaders—Michael

Osheowitz, founder of the nonprofit organization SEO, and John Legere, CEO of T-Mobile—sparked movements to get everyone inside and outside their organizations invested in their disruptive transformation strategies. In Chapter 4, we'll do a deep dive into the four archetypes of disruptive leaders and best practices on how to develop some of the traits and behavior in yourself and in the leaders of your organization.

Element #3: A Culture That Thrives with Disruption

You can have the most beautiful future-customer-focused strategy, along with inspired, disruptive leadership, and still fall flat on your face. Why? If you are like most other incumbents, your culture is geared to sustain the status quo rather than to create disruptive growth. Culture is made up the thousands of ways people work together, share information, make decisions, get things done, and are rewarded or penalized. It guides and influences their attitudes, beliefs, behaviors, and actions. It conveys in subtle ways what the organization values and prioritizes.

To execute your disruptive growth strategy, you need a culture that thrives at the edge of disruption—one where everyone is focused and acts in concert every day to make that transformation happen. The problem for most incumbents is that culture takes years to set in, and it's incredibly difficult to change. I've been told that changing culture is like trying to turn an aircraft carrier.

I've had the privilege of being on an aircraft carrier.[8] I visited the U.S.S. *Nimitz* toward the end of its crew's six-month training process on what is called a "surge" training day, an exercise designed to test the limits of the new five-thousand-member crew. The carrier was going full speed with one hundred planes taking off from the bow and landing on the stern every hour. Three supply ships were sailing alongside with tenuous lines connecting them to the carrier and replenishing food and fuel, one of the most dangerous naval maneuvers. One misstep and disaster would ensue.

In the midst of this intense activity, the captain issued a command to turn the ship. Slowly and carefully, the carrier, the planes, and the support ships all turned in unison. It took almost ten minutes to turn the ship, but it turned. There was no way that at the start of the six-month training, the crew (most of whom were eighteen- and nineteen-year-olds) could have pulled this off. But the captain had trained, drilled, and stretched his crew to the point where he had full confidence that when he gave the command to turn, the ship would turn.

Have you ever tried to get a teenager or young adult, let alone five thousand of them, to do something exactly the way you wanted it done? If you have, then you understand the enormity of the challenge facing the captain. This is the same challenge organizations face when they are trying to change their culture. But like the ship turned, so can an organization's culture.

The organizations featured in this book systematically changed aspects of their culture to keep their people focused on their core objective: creating disruptive transformation and value for future customers. To do this, they examined and redesigned as needed the core beliefs that define who they are and the underlying practices that embody those beliefs. In several cases, they used digital technologies to initiate, support, and measure culture change. Make no mistake: the changes these organizations underwent were gut wrenching and highly contentious. They had to jettison treasured beliefs while adopting new practices and procedures that exposed weaknesses in their talent and leadership.

In Chapter 5, I highlight the three beliefs—openness, ownership, and agility—that transform organizations from being status quo "stuck cultures" into "flux cultures" able to thrive with disruption. And in Chapter 6, I'll explain how to set up your culture operating system— the structure and processes, as well as the stories, symbols, rituals, and traditions that people share with each other—so it hard-wires a flux culture into your organization.

In these chapters, I'll share the stories of Adobe, ING Bank, McKinsey, Nokia, T-Mobile, Southern New Hampshire University, and other organizations in which the three capabilities of disruptive transformation are in sync and support breakthrough growth. Although the success of these companies ought to be celebrated, it's worth remembering that most organizations don't stay disruptive for long. Almost all will eventually fall from the pedestal, and the companies featured in this book will likely not be the exception. Only a few organizations—companies like Southwest Airlines, which has been profitable for forty-five *consecutive* years—have mastered the art of sustained disruptive transformation over decades.

BUILDING DISRUPTIVE TRANSFORMATION STRATEGY

Creating disruptive transformation is a heroic act based on the audacious belief that you and your organization can figure out not only strategic moves to make but also how to lead each other through the messy human side of change. I encourage you to begin that journey now. And the best way to do so is to know where you are starting from and where you are going.

A super-quick exercise can help: Rate your organization's current ability to be disruptive—to challenge the status quo and try to change a situation for the better—in its strategy, leadership, and culture on a scale of 1 (not at all disruptive) to 10 (extremely disruptive). Don't overthink it; just write down a number for each element and then average them.

___ A strategy inspired by future customers to make big gulp decisions

___ Leadership that creates a movement of disruptors

___ A culture that thrives with disruption

___ **Total**

___ **Average** (Total/3): Your organization's disruption quotient score

Take note of your organization's disruption quotient (ODQ). Similar to an IQ test, the ODQ is a proxy for how much disruptive breakthrough growth your organization is capable of creating. But unlike an IQ score, you *can* change your ODQ.

It's important to note that the goal here is not necessarily to have a perfect "10" ODQ. You may be in an industry that doesn't require a high level of disruption. If most organizations in your sector have a ODQ score of 3, then scoring a 4 may be sufficient to find and secure your future growth customer. But you may be vulnerable to another organization that is aiming to operate at the 5 ODQ level. What's more important is to ask how much disruption you and your organization can create and sustain over time. This goes to the heart of your disruptive transformation strategy.

BEGIN WITH THE END IN MIND

My hope is that the stories in this book will help you stay focused on why you want to become a disruptor in the first place: to challenge the status quo to make a situation better. When I started Altimeter in 2008, we disrupted the analyst firm status quo with a business model that made cutting-edge research freely available when everyone else was charging a substantial subscription.[9] We wanted to reach more people with the open research to help leaders thrive with disruption. Building a disruptive business and eventually selling it was tough, hard work, but the focus on the audience impact kept us centered and moving forward with our disruption strategy.

There will be times when the way forward will be illuminated by what feels like a penlight in the dark night. There will be times when you will doubt the course that you have chosen. And there will be times when the entire world seems aligned against you. Use these setbacks as opportunities to learn. Your vision of the future will provide you with the solace, inspiration, and strength to continue.

Never cease believing that what you are doing is worth the pain and confusion that is the natural course of disruption. I wish you all the best in sustaining your disruption mindset and achieving the transformation of your dreams.

"I skate to where the puck is **going to be**, not where it has been."

—Wayne Gretzky, greatest hockey player ever

CHAPTER 1
• • • • • • • • • •

THE SIMPLE SECRET OF SUCCESSFUL DISRUPTIVE STRATEGIES

———————————●———————————

I F THERE's one thing I've learned from being a business and technology analyst for two decades is that it's rarely a new technology that results in breakthrough growth. Google and Facebook didn't introduce the search engine or the social network, respectively; their products were third-generation iterations of technology that already existed.10 Uber didn't use any new technology at all but created a new use for location services. Breakthrough growth is born from an uncanny ability to see the future and direct all of the resources of your organization to chase after it.

For most incumbent organizations, there's just one problem: your familiar, profitable, existing customers. Those customers of today look pretty good. Why on earth would you drop them to go after another group of customers, especially if it's not clear if those new customers actually exist? No, no, executives say. It's much safer and better to stay with what you know.

That status quo thinking is the biggest hurdle to breakthrough growth because that growth isn't likely to come from the customers you have today. Disruptive, exponential growth comes only from your customers of tomorrow. One executive compared the status quo approach to driving by mostly looking at a large rear-view mirror that magnifies the road behind them. No one would ever navigate and drive this way, yet this is how most companies are run. That's because we've been trained to pay attention to and serve our best customers. But that dooms incumbents' attempts to disrupt. While they are busy keeping these "best" customers happy, the less profitable—but nevertheless emerging—customers are being stolen away by competitors and new entrants.

This is the innovator's dilemma that Harvard Business School professor Clay Christensen identified: the inability to give up the easy, familiar profits from the best, existing customers to chase after less profitable customers with new products and innovations.11 Many smart people like Professor Christensen have warned how powerful this pull is and even concluded that because of it, an incumbent organization can never become truly disruptive. And yet I see organizations becoming disruptive happening all the time.

For incumbent organizations that want to become disruptors, the key to transformative growth is to break the chokehold of the profitable "best" customers on the company psyche. The organization needs to see these "best" customers as impermanent, vulnerable to market shifts. It's table stakes to meet their expectations and serve them well. But future growth lies elsewhere—and you need to plan accordingly.

Let's take a look at how one company placed its vision of how to serve a new customer at the center of its entire strategy.

HOW T-MOBILE DISRUPTED THE MOBILE PHONE INDUSTRY

At the end of 2011, T-Mobile was at an impasse. Its proposed merger with AT&T had been quashed due to monopoly concerns. As the distant fourth-place mobile carrier in the United States, there were few options for organic, sustainable growth (see Figure 1.1).[12] T-Mobile had lost $4.7 billion that year on $20.6 billion of revenue.[13] But there was one gleaming piece of good news: the failed merger with AT&T had netted T-Mobile a $3 billion breakup fee.[14] But what should it do with it? What could its leaders do to drive growth?

Fig. 1.1 Wireless Revenues Generated by Major US Telecommunications Providers in 2011

CARRIER	2011 REVENUES
Verizon	$70.2 billion
AT&T	$63.2 billion
Sprint	$27.4 billion
T-Mobile	$20.6 billion

Source: Statistia

The task of answering these questions was a monumental one and it fell to Andrew Sherrard, at the time senior vice president of marketing at T-Mobile and later its CMO.[15] The company was hemorrhaging subscribers, it didn't have the Apple iPhone, and it was behind in rolling out new network technology like 4G LTE. Moreover, the company was demoralized and listless from the failed merger. T-Mobile needed a jump-start with an aggressive growth strategy. As the underdog, it was willing to risk everything and had the freedom to do some radical things. It saw a chance to shift from a defensive to an offensive mindset.

In January 2012, Sherrard started conducting research into alternative positionings for T-Mobile. Core to that work was understanding unmet customer needs as a way to find a space that T-Mobile could own in the competitive landscape.[16] It was not immediately obvious what they should do, and in fact, several options looked as if the company would perform decently without a radical change in course. "We could have been the urban brand. Another was to become a price leader," Sherrard shared. "But none of them felt like they could really change our fortunes that much."

The one idea that Sherrard and his team kept coming back to was to be a customer advocate in a category that had historically ignored them. Customers were tired of inscrutable contracts that locked them in for years and reduced their power to switch to another carrier. So T-Mobile decided to create transparency and trust with customers by ripping up the traditional two-year contract, separating handset costs from monthly service charges.

"That became our mantra," Sherrard recalled. "We were going to be the people who actually listened to customers in a category that was notoriously bad at helping customers." Conventional wisdom held that customers choose their mobile carrier based on network quality and price. With a much smaller network, T-Mobile was betting that customers would choose a better relationship over network size and quality.

This was a big gulp, bet-the-company move. Obliterating the two-year contract exposed T-Mobile customers to being picked off by competitors. Sherrard and his team were also uncertain whether the best customers from AT&T and Verizon would risk defecting to T-Mobile for an inferior network. Would T-Mobile pick up only the least profitable customers from the other carriers?

"We had been bouncing those ideas around for a while, but they felt pretty radical and scary," Sherrard said. "We never had the courage of our convictions to go out and try it in such a holistic way." What convinced them to take the plunge was the extensive customer research they gathered and the financial modeling that showed they could convince AT&T's best (and unhappiest) customers to switch. Indeed, it appeared that customers were fed up with the traditional mobile carriers. Still, there was tremendous trepidation within T-Mobile about the strategy. Sherrard remembers that one executive said to him, "I know we have to jump off the cliff and into the river. I just want to make sure there's water down there."

This all changed when John Legere joined T-Mobile as its new CEO in September 2012. Sherrard's team had originally planned to launch the new pricing plan in August 2013. Legere asked the team to deliver it instead in March, six months earlier than planned. "I don't think we can wait that long," Sherrard recalled Legere saying.

T-Mobile now had an objective—a purpose—that aligned and focused the organization around customer obsession and growth. "It became a thing we lived every day and every week and every month and every quarter," Sherrard shared. "How do we grow it? How are we paying for growth? What other things do we need to do to create savings, so we can drive more growth? Do we have enough new things coming in to fuel the growth that we want this company to have?"

In March 2013, T-Mobile unveiled its "Un-carrier" rebranding with a "no service contract" offer. Three months later, it followed up with an offering that enabled early handset upgrades. Every three months, a new offering came out that addressed another customer pain point— and also drove the news cycle. T-Mobile had mapped out a product or service release every quarter for the next two years (see Figure 1.2).[17] "That was exhausting," Sherrard recalled. "We just kept going and drove a crazy amount of growth those first couple of years. We cut out the pain points for customers and captured their hearts and minds."

The result was disruptive growth. In 2011, T-Mobile had $20.1 billion in revenue, and by the end of 2018, it had a more than doubled to $43.3 billion in revenue, a 11 percent compound annual growth rate (see Figure 1.3).[18] In comparison, Verizon and AT&T wireless revenue grew only 3.9 percent and 1.7 percent, respectively, and Sprint shrank 3 percent.[19] As a result of that growth, T-Mobile increased its share of the US wireless market from 10 percent at the end of 2012 to 19 percent at the end of 2018. And T-Mobile has come full circle. Its transformative growth strategy followed the aftermath of its failed acquisition by AT&T. On April 29, 2018, T-Mobile announced that it was acquiring Sprint Corporation.[20] While the transaction must still clear several regulatory at the time of this writing, it's an indication of how far and how quickly T-Mobile's prospects changed in just a few years.

T-Mobile's growth was rooted in classic disruptive innovation thinking it was laser focused on the unmet needs of customers. At the core of this strategy was not a shiny new technology; T-Mobile's innovation was a simple but powerful pricing model that challenged the industry's standard practices.

Fig. 1.2 Major Milestones of T-Mobile's Un-carrier Rollout, 2013-2016

March 2013	*Simple Choice* – No Service Contracts. 44M subscribers
July 2013	*Jump* – Upgrades for All. 45M subscribers
October 2013	*Simple Global* – free international roaming. 46.7M subscribers
January 2014	*Music Freedom* and *Carrier Freedom* – streaming music doesn't count against data usage and paid off device payments for switchers. 49M subscribers
June 2014	*Test Drive* – Free trial period. 51M subscribers
September 2014	*Wi-Fi Unleashed* – Wi-Fi calling and free texting on Gogo flights. 53M subscribers
December 2014	*Data Stash* – rollover unused data for up to a year. 55M subscribers
March 2015	*Un-carrier for Business* – simplified pricing and 24/7 support. 57M subscribers
November 2015	*Binge On* – Unlimited video streaming. 63M subscribers
June 2016	*T-Mobile Tuesdays* – Weekly promotions every Tuesday. 67M subscribers

Source: T-Mobile

But T-Mobile's strategy also diverged from classic disruption strategy in two ways. First, it challenged the belief that incumbents are unable to radically change the core of the business fast enough to meet emerging customer needs. T-Mobile didn't simply put a pricing model change in place; it rewired every part of its $20 billion business to become the Un-carrier. Second, it did not only go after the less profitable fringe customers of other carriers. The Un-carrier strategy was a full-out assault on the leaders, and especially AT&T, which had the same type of network, making it particularly easy for those subscribers to switch.As a result, T-Mobile didn't just drive growth faster than its competitors did; it also disrupted the wireless carrier industry in the United States, even though it was the fourth-place player and significantly smaller than the leaders, AT&T and Verizon. T-Mobile's no-contract approach shone a bright light on the not-so-customer-friendly practices of the other carriers and forced the entire industry to change. One by one, they dropped their two-year contracts, with AT&T being the last of the four major carriers to give up contracts in early 2016. Today, Americans take for granted features like no contracts, free music and video streaming, and the ability to upgrade their phones whenever they want.

It might be tempting to dismiss T-Mobile's achievement. Given its fourth-place position in the industry, it had nothing to lose, so why not take the risk? But the unyielding pull of the known, of the status quo, is so powerful that day after day, the vast majority of business leaders who can take a similar path to T-Mobile's instead turn away. What T-Mobile did was make the vision of the future customer so compelling and so real that its leaders had no choice but to pursue it. It's a subtle but important difference: the disruption mindset moves leaders and organizations not out of fear and a position of weakness but from a point of view of opportunity and confidence.

Fig. 1.3 Wireless Revenue Generated by Major US Telecommunications Providers, 2011-2017 (in billion US dollars)

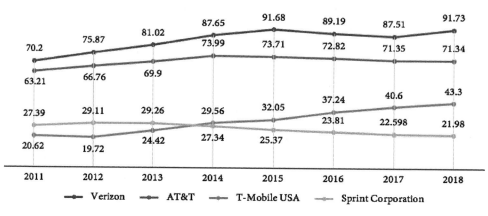

Source: Statistia; AT&T, Sprint, T-Mobile, and Verizon annual reports.

WHO IS YOUR FUTURE CUSTOMER?

As business leaders, we've been taught to design certainty and attainability into our business plans and strategies because that's what we get rewarded for: excellent operational execution. We systematically analyze what went right and what went wrong in the past year and make adjustments for the coming year. We limit our possibilities because we set strategy by looking in the rear-view mirror.

This approach works great if you are in a stable, slow-changing industry where competitors don't rock the boat and potential new entrants stay in their lanes. The last time I checked, there not many industries that fit this description.

As T-Mobile's growth story suggests, what disruptive transformation organizations do exceedingly well is looking confidently into the future to anticipate customer needs that don't exist today. The further into the future they look, the more disruptive they are.

Of course, it is extremely difficult to accurately predict and define the future. That's why most organizations shy away from doing it. *What if we're wrong? What if we head down one path and have to change course?* I'm not asking you to predict the future. Instead, I'm asking that you make an educated guess about *one thing* and one thing only: what you think your future customers are going to need. The more confidence you have in your understanding of those future customers, the more likely you will be to choose to chase after them, even at the expense of today's profitable customers.

In this way, disruption strategy is no different from a traditional strategy. Strategy is simply deciding what you will do and—just as important—what you *will not* do. A disruptive transformation strategy frames that strategic choice specifically. Which customers will be your priority: your customers today or tomorrow? In T-Mobile's case, its leaders staked their future on future customers who wanted a more authentic and transparent relationship with their carrier.

This focus on future customers is the one thing that can act as a counterweight against the certainty of revenues and profits coming from today's customers. How many times have you heard, "We can't pull resources away from serving our best customers" or "There's no time or budget to explore options for the future"? These are the comments of an organization prioritizing today over tomorrow. A focus on future customers is the way to address the classic innovator's dilemma, where easy profits from existing customers blind incumbents from seeingnew competitors inching in, picking off customers on the edges.

HOW FACEBOOK TURNED ITS BACK ON ITS BEST CUSTOMERS

Let's take a walk down memory lane to August 2003, when MySpace was launched as an extension of the music and entertainment website eUniverse. I met with CEO Chris DeWolfe that fall and recall his incredible focus on understanding and serving MySpace's core audience, which at that time was the indy music scene in Los Angeles. With promotion and access to eUniverse's audience, MySpace grew quickly and was acquired in 2005 by News Corp for an astounding $580 million.[21]

In contrast, Mark Zuckerberg started Facebook out of his dorm room in January 2004. At first, the site was open only to Harvard undergrads. After a month in operation, half of all the Harvard undergrads had signed up and were clamoring to connect with their friends at other universities. In March 2004, Facebook expanded to Columbia, Stanford, and Yale and quickly added other universities. A year later, the Facebook team realized that they were reaching saturation of college students: they had to expand. The natural place was to add high school students, which Facebook did in September 2005.

Then on September 26, 2006, Facebook did the unimaginable: it opened up membership to anyone at least thirteen years old with a valid email address.[22] And then to the horror of the college and high school students on Facebook, *their parents* joined Facebook. Obviously, this was not a feature that students would have ever conceivably asked for! Yet Facebook did it because the only way it could grow was to open the site to anyone.

Facebook took the calculated risk of turning its back on its current and best customers—students—in order to could cultivate new relationships with a much bigger market. The company's leaders bet that these students got so much value from being on Facebook that they would put up with their parents' hanging out with them. Facebook also bet that adults would find Facebook as sticky an experience as students did and took controversial steps, like adding the News Feed feature a few weeks prior to opening up the site, to make it more useful and appealing to all audiences.

Meanwhile, what did MySpace do? It doubled down on music and entertainment as the centerpiece of the site because that's what its core—its most important and loyal members—wanted. The professional managers at News Corp—smart, experienced leaders—developed a plan based on the needs of those core members and worked the plan. After all, that was the formula for business success. If the plan wasn't working, then execution must be the problem. There was no room, no space, to deviate from the plan because it was built on sound business fundamentals. Never mind that it was focused on the wrong thing: the audience it had today, the equivalent of skating to where the puck is.

Facebook already knew what its audience wanted today and put most of its efforts into figuring out where it was going, skating in every possible direction to see where the puck was going to be. And here's the crazy thing: Facebook really didn't know with any great certainty where its members were going to be. They made some educated guesses, developed hunches, and had some ideas gleaned from watching and listening closely to their members. And that was okay because they were playing a new game.

This was very evident when Mark Zuckerberg briefed me on Facebook's strategy in 2006. I was one of the first analysts he briefed, and no matter what question I asked, Zuckerberg would always answer with a variation of, "Facebook is a utility." I'd ask what member needs Facebook was prioritizing, and he would reply, "Facebook is a utility … so anything that members need." What about advertising? "Because Facebook is a utility, everyone will use it and advertisers want to reach everyone." Although Facebook was growing and its members loved it, my business side was skeptical that Facebook knew what it was doing.

I was stuck in the plan-and-execute mindset while Facebook was running a new playbook with a disruption mindset. With a singular focus on increasing its members, Facebook surpassed MySpace in monthly visitors in early 2008.[23] MySpace reached its peak of 75 million members in December 2008, when it started declining, and never recovered.[24] Facebook grew from 100 million monthly active users in 2008 to 2.3 billion monthly active users by late 2018.[25]

Facebook, like other disruptive organizations, centered its growth strategy on the fastest-moving part of its entire ecosystem: customers. And not just any customers, but the customers of the future. They confidently looked far into the future to anticipate customer needs that didn't exist then.

In 2016 Mark Zuckerberg unveiled a ten-year road map at the company's annual developers' conference, F8.[26] That road map is a remarkable public view of where Facebook sees future growth coming from that serves to keep the company and its ecosystem of developers focused on how it sees customer needs changing.

One could argue that in light of the many controversies engulfing the company in late 2018 and 2019, Facebook should have taken greater care to listen to the growing chorus of concerns about data, privacy, and Russian meddling. It's also clear that the ten-year road map didn't anticipate Zuckerberg's pivoting Facebook into private social networks.

I've been watching Facebook since it started, and the one thing I've been struck by is how Zuckerberg has continually and steadfastly reinvented himself as well as Facebook. That willingness to face the reality of the present while focusing on the future enables Facebook to remain dominant and disruptive.

YOU HAVE THE ADVANTAGE IF YOU FOCUS ON FUTURE CUSTOMERS

There are so many things about the future that you cannot control, from what the economy will do to the emergence of new technologies and competitors. The one and only thing that you can completely control is what you choose to focus on. All of your organization's energy and resources need to be focused on understanding, identifying, and meeting the needs of your future customer. If you can do this, you have a huge advantage over less focused incumbents as well as start-ups.

That's right, incumbents have numerous advantages, but they must be tuned to chasing after future customers and not preserving the status quo. These advantages include:

Customers. Having the ability to sell to an existing customer who already trusts you is a huge advantage over start-ups that have zero customer base. A subset of your existing customers will likely be your future customers as well, but you must be ready to let them jump over to the new offering, which may result in lower revenue and profits per customer. If you don't, you make yourself vulnerable to someone else who will.

Brand. It's far easier to introduce a new product with an existing brand versus a brand that no one has heard of, as most start-ups have to do. New products and services don't necessarily have to have a new brand; they could be a sub-brand or morph into a house of brands. But it can be tricky evolving the brand to meet future customer needs. T-Mobile leveraged its brand equity and awareness but also had to overcome a legacy of poor quality and poor coverage with existing and former customer by repositioning itself as the "Un-carrier."

Talent. An incumbent can move talented, experienced people into the new business and give them resources. If they are truly focused on serving future customers, they will be entrepreneurial in finding inventive ways to meet them where they are. Start-ups have to recruit people in a tough talent market, with little cash and lots of options in an iffy venture.

Scale. Backend processes, from sales operations and customer service to HR and finance, provide the infrastructure for effective operations. Start-ups have to build these from scratch. But scale can become a liability if these processes atrophy over time rather than constantly evolve. When T-Mobile began its transformation, it made sure that all aspects of the business supported the Un-carrier experience, from how people were greeted in stores to how phone calls were handled .

Cash. An incumbent can use cash from existing cash-positive businesses to plow into new, less profitable customer segments. Start-ups have to raise money. Cash is also the backup plan: if all else fails and a start-up does break through to address a customer need that you didn't catch, buy the start-up.

A strategy that focuses on future customers frees an incumbent organization to be able to use all of its assets and scale to go after that customer. This is one of the reasons the biggest disruptive players, like Amazon, Apple, Facebook, Google, and Netflix, keep getting bigger. They have the scale, brand, customer relationships and cash to continually reinvest in the engine that drives new growth initiatives.

> # "Change is the law of life. And those who look only to the past or present are certain to miss the future."
>
> —John F. Kennedy

BEST PRACTICES TO FOCUS ON FUTURE CUSTOMER NEEDS

To orient a disruptive growth strategy around future customers, you need to systematically and intentionally build an obsession about customers, and especially future customers, into the DNA of your organization. That focus must be ingrained into every person and every process. Your organization must have a way to identify emerging customer needs from the edges, empowering the people who serve customers every day to have their observations matter. And there must be a process that evaluates these data points with fresh eyes and an open heart to seeing what you may not want to hear.

There is no secret sauce for doing this. But there are a few best practices that disruptive organizations use to make future customers part of their agenda every day.

Put Customers in Your Dashboards

Not too long ago, I helped the executive team of a consumer products company create an organizational and culture strategy to support their digital transformation. At one of our workshops, we had just finished discussing the need to be more customer obsessed when I asked the CEO what was on the top left-hand corner of his dashboard. He sheepishly replied, "Inventory turns."

You are what you measure.

Take a look at your personal dashboard, and see where and how customers are represented. Are they even there? If customers are in your dashboard already, bravo! Now go a level deeper: How are they represented? Do you have mainly what I call "vanity metrics"—things like counting revenues, products sold, number of customers? Or do you include meaningful "relationship metrics"—things like lifetime value, customer satisfaction, and loyalty. And finally, is your future customer represented on your dashboard?

A few years ago, I got a good look at a screen capture of Mark Zuckerberg's dashboard from March 2010, and it was a revelation. The first column had typical customer metrics: number of registered users; average daily, weekly, and monthly users; number of new users; and so on. It was the second column that was very interesting. Titled "Mobile Usage," it tracked mobile usage by platform. This was March 2010, when there were only 100 million mobile users of Facebook and half of them used the mobile web version, not an app. But Zuckerberg already knew that mobile would be a big part of Facebook's future and devoted the appropriate space on his dashboard to follow these emerging new users.

What I love about this practice is that you don't need to be an executive to make it happen. Anyone with a dashboard and access to some basic reporting can do it. You don't even have to capture quantitative data; you can create a feed of what customers are saying about your product on social media. Even internal functions can do this. One finance team I came across measured the net promoter score both internally with employees as well as after interactions with customers, accounts receivables, and accounts payables.

Determine what customer metrics or information matter most to your current and future success. Then carve out some space on your dashboard to put your customers front and center so that you make them the focus of your agenda every day.

Spark Curiosity About Customers

One of the biggest problems I have encountered in the organizations I've worked with is that people in general, and leaders in particular, do not think they have permission to think about the future. They've been told that achieving the monthly, quarterly, and annual goals is of paramount importance. They've been told to keep their heads down and focused on the work right in front of them. No one has ever told them to be curious, to ask why customers do the things that they do, or to ask why the organization does things the way it does.

What a waste.

Your employees, and especially those who interact with customers every day, have firsthand knowledge of what's really going on with customers. Digital collaboration platforms can quickly spread that knowledge to the top echelons of the organization. Your employees become the early warning system of emerging customer needs. But this happens only if you systematically and intentionally give permission to your people to be curious about customers and build a structure into the fabric of the organization that allows them to do so.

One of the best ways to spark curiosity about customers is to create empathy maps for your current and future ones. I first came across a formal, scalable way to build empathy maps at an IBM Design Thinking workshop in 2014.[27] The idea behind these maps is to develop a common understanding of your customers' goals and motivations based on observable data and examples. A simple framework guides the collection and synthesis of those data—what the person says, does, thinks, and feels (see Figure 1.4).[28]

Fig. 1.4 **Example of an Empathy Map**

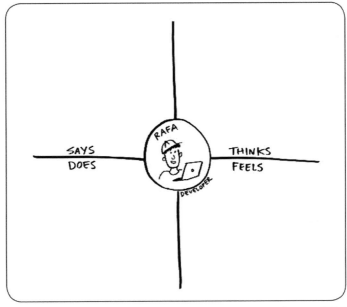

Source: IBM

Ask your team to gather examples of what customers say, do, think, and feel for different types of customers. You can collect these examples from formal interviews, focus group sessions, or informal observations from listening in on call center calls. Write each example or observation on a single sticky note, and put it into the appropriate quadrant. The process of creating the empathy map will reveal where there is a common understanding of your customers within your team, where there is divergence, and where there are gaping holes.

Repeating this process for future customers is even more challenging because you'll likely be grappling with a lot of blank space. But that space will fuel curiosity among your employees and prompt them to be on the lookout for examples of what an emerging customer says, does, thinks, and feels. Those "data" will help build out empathy maps of future customers.

There are a few pitfalls to watch out for when being curious about customers. First, understand that you and your employees are not the customers. You must put aside your personal preferences and biases and see the world as they see it. That's what empathy is all about: being able to walk in their shoes. With time, you will begin to see current and future customers as real people with a complex set of values, hopes, fears, and behaviors.

Second, be aware that this isn't about making personas or segments, that is, well-researched models or simplified representations of your customers used to develop journey maps and marketing execution. Personas and customer segments require a high degree of certainty but a narrow range of focus. Empathy maps do just the opposite: they encourage the development of complexity and contradictions and highlight, for example, how a customer may think something but say something different. If done correctly, empathy maps should make you even more curious to learn more about your fascinating customers.

Create a Customer Advisory Board

I'm frequently asked by small and medium-sized companies that lack the hefty customer research budgets large organizations have what they can do to better understand customers. My answer is to form a customer advisory board (CAB) that can provide you with insight and feedback on what you are doing well and what you could be doing better.

Don't stack the CAB with your biggest and best current customers. Instead find the customers who push you to do things in a different way. Ask your sales and customer service teams who the most insightful customers are, the ones that challenge the way your company works. These customers will hold you to a higher standard and have higher expectations. They are well versed in what the competition offers. And they frequently want something new, something customized that you don't currently offer. You do your best to accommodate them, but they don't ever seem to be completely satisfied.

You might find these people among the ranks of your current customers. But they could also be prospects or customers you've lost. The key is to deepen your relationship with people who are the best representatives of what you believe your future customers will be like.

If you can build your CAB to represent your future customers, you will have at your disposal an instant focus group to test out new ideas. While you may need to take some antacids before you attend a CAB meeting, I guarantee you that a strong CAB will push you further and faster than anything else that you can come up with. In fact, I would argue that it's more important to listen to your CAB than your board of directors because you ignore the voice of your future customers at your peril. Having concrete examples of what future customers want is a powerful antidote to stuck-in-today thinking.

Find Your Customer-obsessed Staff

Similar to your CAB, seek out the people in your organization who are already naturally inclined to think about your customers. You likely already know who they are. They frequently point out ways that the organization could change to be more customer friendly. They walk in customers' shoes and intuitively understand their pain points. They take the customer's side on things. And they are naturally curious about and eager to solve customer problems. And, yes, they can be a thorn in your side as they advocate for change.

When you find these customer-obsessed people (COPs), give them the social proof that their opinions not only matter but are being heard and making a difference. For example, one organization routinely highlights call center staff at monthly team meetings who not only surfaced a problem from a service call but also took the initiative to push through a change in product or policy. Recognizing the advocacy that addresses a customer's needs turns that person into a hero to be emulated, encouraging others to surface the voices of customers.

You can also invite your COPs to meet with your CAB, having parallel meetings to double the impact on your executives and organization. As you pull your disruptive transformation strategy together, engage these COPs to vet and advance your plan. Not only will they push you to be even more customer focused, you will be bringing them into your strategic thinking so that they can be on the lookout for data and examples to confirm or refine the strategy.

Define Your Future Customer With Research, Not Hearsay

Recently I participated in a client workshop where the objective was to kick off a project that would define the company's customer of the future. My colleague started the day off by asking everyone to draw a picture of an alien. It didn't matter what kind of alien. He encouraged us to draw whatever came to mind, and we posted the pictures all around the room. There were the usual big blob-headed aliens, ones with eighteen arms and legs, and so on. Looking at these, it was obvious that we all had a different idea of what an alien looked like and we had all come into the room with preconceived notions of what an alien looks like based on the movies we've seen or the books we've read.

We did this exercise to illustrate that trying to define a future customer is like trying to draw an alien: we all come at it from a different perspective and have a different vision of who that customer is. We hadn't yet spent the time and energy to systematically explore what that future customer would look like, intentionally narrow down the options, and align on a common understanding. All too often, we want a quick and easy answer to help us move from a place of uncertainty to a place of certainty, so we pull from our past experiences.

Instead, consider a different process—one where you first gather in a room to discuss the questions that need to be answered to define the future customer. Focus not on what you already know about today's customer but what you don't know about your future customer. This is what T-Mobile did with research. Instead of asking customers what they wanted today, they asked those customers what made them unhappy about their relationship with their mobile carrier, and in that way, they began to get some ideas about what their future customer might look like. Doing deep narrative research may seem like an unnecessary, costly, and time-consuming step. But almost every disruptive company I have studied made a deep investment in making sure that a common and consistent definition of future customers was clearly understood and accepted throughout the organization.

One pushback that I get from clients is that Apple famously didn't do customer research. That's true. They did not put much stock on doing focus groups and surveys with today's customers because they believe they can't tell you much about tomorrow's customers. But Apple is famously customer obsessed, especially about understanding unmet underlying needs. They would find a problem that didn't work well—for example, being unable to carry your music with you—and designed a music player that put "1000 songs in your pocket."

Doing deep, meaningful research is a serious investment, and it may be difficult to secure funding when the organization and its executives are wired to focus on the short term. Here's a way to win over skeptical executives: commit them to a half-day where the objective will be to walk out the door with a clear view of the future customer the company will serve. I guarantee you that the leaders in the room will be very uncomfortable with this charge!

The actual goal of this half-day exercise, however, isn't to come up with the final answer but to highlight the need to have a process that builds a model of the future customer. By forcing the team to craft a future customer profile, you will identify glaring gaps about what you don't know and what you still need to learn. Turn the attention to gathering that information and setting aside the people and resources to fill those gaps.

Developing a vision of the future customer is darn hard, to be sure. We'd rather deal with the knowable and the known, the customers of today, than engage in the deep work these practices require. We perceive there is much at risk, for the company and for ourselves, to fathom the possibility of alternative futures and to pick one to pursue.

THE PITFALLS OF FOCUSING ON FUTURE CUSTOMERS

Focusing on future customers comes with some potential dangers and pitfalls that must be avoided. You might become enamored with one particular vision of a future customer and fail to listen to warning signs that you are on the wrong track. Or you might move too quickly to chase after the future customers and not tend to the needs of current customers. Before I close this chapter, I'll share a cautionary tale of getting too far ahead of yourself and your customers.

Netflix today is one of the hottest companies around. Not only is it a beloved international brand with its original content and streaming services, its stock has also been a darling of Wall Street through most of 2018, almost doubling in price in twelve months.[29] But Netflix almost didn't survive its own efforts to drive disruptive growth.

Contrary to popular belief, cofounder Reed Hastings did not start Netflix because of forty dollars in late fees. He and cofounder Marc Randolph simply wanted to be the "Amazon.com of something."[30] In 1999 after several false starts, they came across one approach that seemed to stick: a DVD subscription plan with no due dates or late fees. They coupled this subscription plan with the ability to add movies to a queue, and it was a hit with customers. Following this success, Netflix launched its streaming service in early 2007 with only a thousand movie titles.[31]

As their subscribers increased and streaming became a larger portion of their business, Netflix looked at the data and realized DVD rentals were peaking and streaming was the way forward. Competition was also heating up. Although Blockbuster was fading, new entrants like Hulu, Amazon, and Google were getting into the streaming video space. CEO Reed Hastings became concerned with how to navigate the "innovator's dilemma" and shift Netflix's business model. The company anticipated needing to phase out the less profitable DVD rental business so it could focus on its streaming and acquiring new and better content.[32] Yet they knew that few companies rarely succeed at making a pivot as big as this.

In July 2011, Netflix announced that it would separate streaming from its DVD rental business. By all accounts, this made a lot of sense: Netflix could manage the DVD rental business for decline while using streaming to replace the revenues in the context of emerging fierce competition. In addition, the company announced a price increase: subscriptions would change from $10 a month for DVD rentals and unlimited streaming to $15.98 a month for both or $7.99 per month for either service as a stand-alone subscription.[33] A few months later, they announced that the new DVD rental service would be named "Qwikster."[34]

The reaction from customers was swift and damning. Subscribers hated it.[35] Twitter hate rained down on Hastings and Netflix. The once-beloved consumer brand was declared damaged beyond repair, with its customer trust in tatters. Netflix hadn't anticipated how much people still loved the red envelopes, even if they just wanted to have the option to rent them. After two tortuous months, 800,000 subscribers had dropped Netflix, and its stock price fell by almost 50 percent, a loss of almost $1 billion in enterprise value.[36]

In September of that year, Hasting wrote a blog post apologizing for the confusion and miscues, opening with an apology: "I messed up. I owe everyone an explanation."[37] Hastings realized that he was trying to do too much at the same time: raising prices while simultaneously separating the business into two companies. More important, he realized that he had not explained the changes adequately to his loyal customers. They felt betrayed by the changes and particularly affronted by having the brand name of their beloved red envelopes changes to Qwikster. By all accounts, it was a rare executive admission of arrogance and hubris, and it would mark the start of the long, slow march toward recovery.

"We weren't going to find an idea or gesture that would make people love us again overnight," Hastings recalled. "We had to earn their trust by being very steady and disciplined. And we had to be careful because we were on probation."[38] First, Netflix quickly killed off the short-lived new brand Qwikster and kept the two offerings under the Netflix brand. Then it resisted the urge to come up with a bright shiny object, like offering a pay-per-view service or buying a company like Roku, which makes streaming TV players. Instead they exercised tremendous discipline by remaining focused on the future of streaming video.

And it worked. In the fourth quarter of 2012, Netflix had added 2 million streaming subscribers, thanks to consumers buying tablets and smart TVs over the holidays.[39] Then in February 2013, it announced an original series, *House of Cards*, which Netflix created based on intersectional data on what would appeal to the most subscribers.[40] The combination of operational excellence, a focus on the future streaming customers' needs and content, and customer lock-in thanks to personalized recommendations led to Netflix's dominance in the space. In mid-2018, Netflix had 130 million streaming subscribers with more than half of those outside the United States.[41]

Netflix got lucky—very lucky. It skated on the brink of disaster as it tried to pivot to pursue disruptive growth. Strategically, its leaders were doing the right thing. But they were so consumed with making the disruptive change that they lost sight of who their customer was, misjudging how fast customers were moving toward streaming. Worse, Netflix's leaders reacted slowly to customer rage. Blinded by their own pursuit of this future change, they couldn't see and react to customers who stood in the way of their perceived right path forward.

The lesson Netflix quickly learned and continues to practice to this day is that you have permission to reach forward and move fast—as long as you continue to earn and secure the trust of your customers every single day. It's a tough balancing act, but Netflix was able to do both by leveraging their core strengths as the incumbent—huge scale and a captive customer base—and then doubled down on execution. With those fundamentals in place, Netflix could disrupt at scale with original programming, culminating in its recent Oscar nomination for best picture with *Roma*. It's an extraordinary journey for any company, and all the more so knowing how close Netflix skated to the brink of disaster.

MOVING FORWARD

In your quest to pursue disruptive transformation, you must develop a compelling vision of where your future customers will be and align the resources of your organization in pursuit of that uncertain future. At the same time, you must continue to execute and deliver in the present day, serving your current customers well without being anchored by them. This is the nuance and power of the disruption mindset: to be able to hold a vision of the future intact while laying the groundwork for it today.

TAKEAWAYS

- Disruptive growth comes from identifying and serving the needs of future customers, not today's customers. A strategy to drive disruptive growth aligns the entire organization to identifying and addressing the needs of future customers.
- Organizations like T-Mobile, Facebook, and Netflix continually focus on understanding those needs, even at the risk of alienating their existing customers.
- To get started, ensure that customer obsession is built into everything that your organization does.

"The reason that God was able to create the world in seven days is that he didn't have to worry about the installed base."

—Enzo Torresi, tech entrepreneur and business leader

CHAPTER 2:

. . . .

PREPARING FOR
THE BIG GULP MOMENT

─────────────●─────────────

I N MY conversations with organizations trying to adopt a disruptive growth and transform themselves, I find that many stop just shy of jumping in. They know that they have to change, but the change is so daunting, the implications so overwhelming, that they stop rather than move forward.

None of the leaders I talked to said that their disruptive transformation process was easy or straightforward. Instead, they described how hard it was, how much time they spent agonizing over the choices, war rooms covered with scenario calculations, and seemingly endless efforts to get everyone aligned. In the end, there was a gut-wrenching moment when they had to say no or take a big gulp and make the call to move forward.

If you want to create meaningful transformative change, I can guarantee that you will not have all of the answers and that not everyone will be in 100 percent agreement when it is time to make a final decision. In that moment, you will need to make the best bet that you can, given what you know at that time. And even after you've made the decision, the rest of your organization and your ecosystem will need to be brought along and convinced that this is the way forward.

So how do you prepare yourself and your organization for that inevitable big gulp moment? Over the years, I have observed many organizations make the call, and they all followed some variation of the following three-step strategy blueprint that you too can follow to prepare for your big gulp moment:

- Build the case with rigorous research.
- Secure buy-in with transparency.
- Burn the boats so that there's no turning back.

Being prepared for your big gulp moment is, above all, about confronting the reality of how hard disruptive transformation is and fully embracing the messy humanness of change rather than covering it up with slogans and workshops (or what I call transformation theater).

BUILD THE CASE WITH RIGOROUS RESEARCH

It was 2010, and Mala Sharma had a major problem. As vice president of product marketing for Adobe's biggest and most profitable product line, Creative Suite, she was given a seemingly impossible task: shifting the business model from packaged software to subscription without killing the business in the process. Adobe dominated the professional creative software market with $2 billion in revenue in just this one category of the business. But Creative Suite, which included such popular software as Photoshop, Acrobat, InDesign, and Illustrator, was also close to saturating the addressable market. There were only so many people willing to pay up to $2,499 for packaged software.

Three key indicators of the business's health were particularly worrisome: (1) revenue growth came mostly from price increases, with virtually no growth in new users outside of education; (2) fast-changing customer needs were not being met because software updates were limited to update release cycles every eighteen to twenty-four months; and (3) Adobe had very little recurring revenue, making it vulnerable to changes in customer demand as the recent recession had proven.

A cloud-based subscription model would address these three issues. Price points would come down and open new markets. New features could be rolled out at any time. And Adobe would have a direct relationship with customers for the first time, enabling not just a revenue stream but also direct knowledge of how they actually used the product.

While Adobe's leaders could see the potential, they had to overcome three major hurdles. First, moving to a subscription model meant that everything about the business had to change, from the way Adobe sold the product (ditching its two-tier distributor/retail model for a direct to customer one on www.adobe.com) to the way it developed products on a much faster time line. Even the finance department had to shift to account for subscription revenue every month instead of recognizing revenue all at once at point of sale. Adobe had to shift to a new business model while supporting the old one during a transition period. Nothing could fail.

Second, Sharma knew that Adobe's top line revenue would decline as people shifted from a large upfront purchase that could be recognized all in the same quarter, to monthly payments that were spread out over time. This compression of revenues would take from twenty-four to thirty-six months to work through as customers gradually switched from packaged software to online subscriptions. Because Adobe is a publicly traded company, declining revenues and profits were bad for its stock prices. And because Adobe was already trading lower against historical averages because of its slower growth, a significant decline in stock price could trigger a takeover bid.

Third, and probably the hardest hurdle to overcome, was that customers were not asking for a subscription-based product. They were happy with the existing packaged software. Yet Sharma and the team at Adobe knew that they were not meeting customers' needs fast enough. More content was being consumed on the Web, creative professionals needed to reinvent themselves and build skills to create for the Web, and Adobe's release cycle couldn't keep up with the fast-changing environment. Sharma and the leadership team believed that Adobe would be in a much stronger position to deliver a better customer experience and drive new growth for the company if they made this drastic move—and survived the change.

The risks were very real. Sharma knew that if she didn't get this right, Adobe would suffer the fate of other incumbents that failed to transform: declining market share, declining profits, and declining prospects. "While I wasn't alone at a personal level, I felt the weight of Adobe's future on my shoulders every day," Sharma admitted.[42]

She decided to first address the issue of customer demand and worked closely with Dave Burkett, the vice president and general management of pricing strategy at Adobe, to test the concept. Adobe tested the subscription model in Australia, with the simple test of a $99 per month offering of Creative Suite Design Premium, the $1,799 suite of tools for Web and print design. At the time, there was nothing new or different about the product other than the payment schedule, which was essentially the same pricing given the eighteen-month average lifetime of the customer. But it tested the viability of attracting a new audience unwilling to pay the large upfront costs of a perpetual model.

The results were encouraging: one-third of the subscription customers were completely new to Adobe because the lower price point allowed them to buy into Adobe's full offering program. And of the existing customers who moved over to the subscription model, half would have simply put up with their existing perpetual product and not upgraded.

Carefully constructing the Australia test was crucial to making the decision to move forward with their strategic plan and securing Adobe executives' support. The test allowed them to literally see the future in concrete terms. They could begin imagining all of the future opportunities that such a shift could bring. They began to believe in their heart and soul that this shift represented the future of the company.

After months of deep research and conversation with the internal pricing team, the strategy team, and finance, Sharma was ready for the final strategic review of the plan. She had met frequently with Adobe's CEO, Shantanu Narayen, and the rest of the executive team, working across departments to answer all of their questions and concerns. The pricing had been modeled to show that the financials would work. The test in Australia had shown that customers responded well to the new offerings. Sales was on board with a plan that would essentially change everything that they did. It was time to make the decision. "There's only so much math you can do," Sharma recalled. "It was the 'hold our hands' moment and it was about having conviction that this is the right thing to do."

They would need that resolve and conviction because a long, tough slog lay ahead of them.

Building Your Case for Disruptive Transformation

I often hear from leaders that their disruptive transformation plans get rejected, but closer examination reveals that the plans had so many holes in them that there was no way anyone would ever bet the company on them. What impressed me most about Sharma and her team is that they took the time to build the case for this huge strategic move carefully. If you want to make a solid case for your disruption strategy, here are a few things to keep in mind:

Invest the resources and time needed. Adobe pulled their top people into the project, starting with the person who owned the existing product, Mala Sharma. The importance and urgency were clearly conveyed, and, more important, the team was given the time and resources to do this right. Depending on how disruptive your ambitions are, you will need to set your time line and investment horizon in terms of months, if not years. Plan and set expectations accordingly.

Secure the right data about your future customers. In our conversations, Adobe's leaders shared over and over again how important the data from the Australia test were in changing the hearts and minds of everyone in the organization. The data weren't conclusive or comprehensive, but until then, Adobe's leaders couldn't really imagine what the future could look like. You will need a reference point of customer needs for your deliberations—a centering truth that everyone can look to for inspiration as well as a reality check.

Find champions within your organization. Your case will be more robust and battle tested the more you can get other people and departments to help you build the case. At some point, your top executive will go around the room and poll executives to see what they think about the disruption strategy. If they've had a hand in creating it, your proposal will stand a better chance of acceptance.

Let's dig deeper into how to move from building the case to getting buy-in for it. After all, you are asking people to take a gigantic uncertain step into the future. The data, research, and planning you put into building your case appeal to the logical "head" of people. Now let's focus on how to appeal to their emotional "heart" side.

GET BUY-IN WITH TRANSPARENCY AND DIALOGUE

During times of great change and uncertainty, there is a surfeit of distrust created and compounded by shifting power relationships. Change often comes with a shift in reporting relationships and even organizational structure. Employees and partners think, *What will I be doing when the company is transformed? How will my job or influence change as a result? Will the work I've done for the past few years or even decade—all my efforts—be invalidated? How can I trust that this change will end with a good result for me?*

In the course of my research, I found that organizations were able to get through disruptive transformation and maintain trust with their employees, customers, partners, and investors thanks to transparency and dialogue.

The major reason people do not buy into a coming change is that they feel uncertain and unsure what this will mean to them. If they can't understand the change, why it's happening, and how it might affect them, you can't have a discussion with them. But if they understand it, even if they don't like it, you can at least have a discussion and try to come to an agreement.

Transparency builds trust because it leads to accountability on all sides. For example, if you unveil your transformation strategy and its potential impact, both positive and negative, you enter into a conversation and relationship with the other party. Being open about each party's hopes, fears, and the realities that everyone will face during the transformation helps to dispel any perceptions that the person leading the transformation has hidden motivations. Transparency also requires commitment to a shared truth and purpose, which, once decided on, creates accountability to each other to execute on it.

But most often, executives fear being challenged, so they never even approach the conversation, torpedoing efforts before the start. Or they focus on perfecting a one-way message that they will hope will move hearts and minds rather than committing to having a two-way dialogue to build understanding and trust.

What differentiates companies that have successfully adopted disruptive transformation strategies is that they commit to building a relationship through open communication from the start, regardless of the outcome. For Adobe, that meant committing to complete transparency, internally and then externally, from day one.

The real work began when Adobe decided to go forward with Creative Cloud. Everything had to change, from the way they developed products to how they accounted for monthly revenue transactions in finance, to how sales was compensated because they no longer sold to distributors or retailers but directly to customers. And Adobe.com had to shift from being a marketing site to being the product itself because the website was where customers began and continued their relationship with Adobe.

The hardest part of the transition was getting people internally to define success in a new way, shifting from revenues to units and subscribers because everything operationally and financially was geared to revenues from boxed software. To keep everyone across the company aligned, Sharma published a daily decision log after her daily stand-up meeting, intended to create transparency throughout the organization.

Internal acceptance was a significant issue for Adobe, especially for the product team, because they anticipated users would be in full revolt. Sharma worked closely with internal influencers; she sat down with them before the launch and got their commitment to be part of the process. She and her team reached out to community leaders and influencers to convince them about the value of Creative Cloud and also hear their concerns. They also conducted a worldwide in-person tour that touched over thirty thousand people. Transparency about the rough road ahead allowed the Adobe teams to trust each other during and after the launch as they listened to users and made adjustments in the product and pricing to address customer needs.

Adobe was also very focused on creating transparency and trust with the investment community. In November 2011 Adobe was ready to announce the change to the subscription model. Adobe's CFO at the time, Mark Garrett, was tasked with the job of telling Wall Street analysts that revenues and profits would have to decline before the business was rebuilt and would grow again.

It's worth stopping for a second to consider just how bold—and crazy—this was. Organizations tell me all the time that they abandoned their disruptive growth strategies because of the short-term hits their financials would take. Their investors would never accept that.

Adobe was testing the boundaries of how well it could help Wall Street understand the new business. The key was transparency into how the financials would look, that is, into how bad it would get before it got better. "What we said to the investor community was that for the next several years, do not look at our P&L because it's not going tell you anything about the health of the company," Garrett recalled. "What I want you to look at instead is the buildup of the number of subscribers, the average revenue per user per month, and the resulting annualized recurring revenues [ARR]."[43]

Before the markets opened the day it announced the change, Adobe issued a long press release that explained the new business model and laid out the new financial metrics in detail. When Garrett stepped onstage, the financial analysts had already had time to read and absorb the news, allowing Garrett to focus on addressing their concerns rather than managing the announcement itself.

"We held the hand of the analysts, explaining that even though our revenues would be lower next quarter, that it was for a really good reason, namely that people were buying subscriptions quicker than we thought," explained Mike Saviage, the investor relations vice president at Adobe.[44] Adobe also gave investors a way to convert ARR back to the old income statement so that they could get comfortable with the new metrics. Garrett recalled encouraging the finance team to give more numbers and guidance to analysts during this time, saying, "An analyst is not going to buy your stock if they can't model your business."

About a year after that launch announcement, Adobe had a better understanding of how the business would change. It then provided financial analysts a forecast for the number of subscribers and ARR. "We went out on a limb and put out a three-year model showing how we were going to get the business back to where it used to be so that investors could see the light at the end of the tunnel," Garrett shared.

Hitting those quarterly numbers was far from easy. Adobe had to listen to customers, channel partners, and sales reps who were all grappling with a new way to do business with the company. But quarter after quarter, Sharma and her team set and hit the quarterly subscriber numbers and ARR forecasts. And over time, it became easier to forecast because their dashboard was tracking actual consideration and usage.

Meeting the financial targets every quarter established credibility with Wall Street analysts. Wall Street responded well because of the accountability that Adobe's transparency created. Seemingly miraculously, as revenues and profits went down, the stock price *went up* (see Figure 2.1). "We would miss our revenue targets for the quarter but give them new subscribers numbers, which we hit or exceeded," Saviage shared. "The stock was going up while we were missing our revenue numbers, which is completely contrary to everything I've ever learned in investor relations."

Fig. 2.1 Index of Adobe's Revenues, Net Income, and Stock Price, Q4 2011–Q1 2014

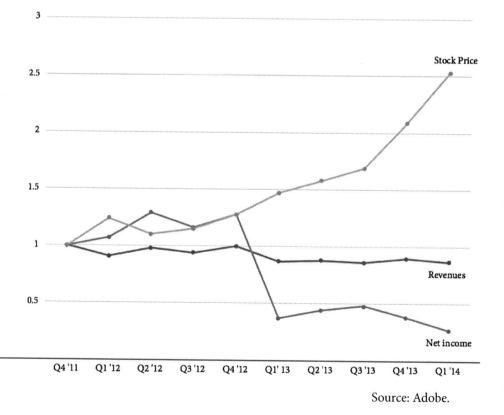

Source: Adobe.

How to Foster Transparency

As we saw with Adobe, it took a lot of vision to formulate its transformation strategy and guts to be forthright with customers, employees, and investors about the coming change. As you contemplate your disruptive transformation strategy, your first instinct may be to back away from the plan because of its audacity, its implications in challenging the status quo. You may be thinking, *There's no way I can say/do/think that.* Rather than turn away, I encourage you to dig deeper into those assumptions. Why can't you be honest and transparent about the change? Why do you think people can't handle the news? Here are some ways you can foster transparency throughout your disruptive transformation:

Invest in relationships, culture, and values long before the change. Sharma said that one of the drivers of Adobe's transformation success is that it had long invested in its culture, which she summed up as "where the most important assets go home every night, where great ideas can come from anywhere, and where people would want to come to work and be their best selves."[45] She repeated these values to herself, her team, and the many people she engaged with throughout the transformation, a reminder of the common values that gave each person a voice in the process. As you prepare for your disruptive transformation, look at the values of your organization. How can they be of service in the journey ahead? It will be a long, tough road, and being able to link the changes you are making back to core values of the organization will be a significant asset that you can draw on. In Chapter 5, I discuss in greater detail how to create a culture where openness and transparency thrive.

Create structure for the uncertain future. Redundancies and layoffs are almost always an inevitable and unfortunate part of disruptive transformation. Rather than try to avoid talking about this reality, you are better off being open about the fact that people will have to be let go so as to minimize uncertainty. For example, in the midst of Nokia's decline as a handset manufacturer, it established the Bridge Program in 2011, which transitioned eighteen thousand employees across thirteen countries to new careers by helping them find new jobs, train for new professions, or set up their own companies.[46] In Finland alone, four hundred new companies were created by around five hundred entrepreneurs. Knowing that such a program existed to provide a professional bridge to the next career move relieved stress and uncertainty for both leaders and employees, and thus allowed the leaders to focus more on the company's transformation and their next step, respectively.[47] As you plan your transformation strategy, identify where such structure would help ease anxiety about an uncertain future and take steps to offer clarity and transparency where possible.

Have uncomfortable discussions now. What are the uncomfortable discussions that you are leaving on the table out of fear of where it could take you or the other person? What issues with key relationships remain unresolved—for example, past slights or misunderstandings? Before you begin your transformation journey, make sure that all of your key relationships are strong and stable, with nothing left unresolved. Nothing can stand in the way of cohesion, unity, and transparency as you begin this journey.

BURN THE BOATS

In 334 B.C., at the tender age of twenty-one, Alexander the Great set out to conquer the formidable Persian Empire, ruled by Darius III. Alexander sailed a fleet of 120 ships across the narrow Hellespont Strait into enemy territory. He knew that his men were outnumbered five to one, but he could sense victory. His first order to his captains: "Burn the boats." Confused, his men asked why they should destroy the one thing that could take them safely home. Alexander answered, "We will go home in Persian ships or we will die here." They went on to conquer Persia.[48]

When organizations go through disruptive transformation, there are many dark days when people will pine for the "golden days" and wish for things to go back to the way they were. As long as there is a possibility to go back, you can't really move forward together. As long as there is a hope that executives might give up and reverse course, your employees, customers, and partners won't fully commit—or worse, they will actively fight the change.

This is where disruptive transformation and change management differ. When you aim for disruptive transformation, the road ahead is so difficult that you must commit yourself and your organization completely. There can be no turning back. There must be total and utter conviction that the path forward is the only one to take.

When Adobe launched the subscription product Creative Cloud, the boxed product Creative Suite was still in the market. Running both was a hedge against subscriptions failing and also provided time for the company to create and test a robust product. Also, Adobe hadn't yet made the significant back office changes needed to support Creative Cloud at scale. But with each successful quarter, they became more confident that subscriptions would work.

By May 2013, Creative Cloud had half a million subscribers and was ready to commit itself to a cloud-based future.[49] At the Adobe Max conference, customers gathered, expectantly waiting for product announcements about the next software release of Creative Suite 7. Instead, Adobe announced that those new features would be available only through Creative Cloud and that the current version, Creative Suite 6, would not be updated.[50]

It had been only a year since Creative Cloud had been launched, and the announcement took the audience and customers around the world by surprise. "This was our 'burn the boats' moment," Adobe CFO Mark Garrett remembered. "We were most worried about the people who had bought the boxed product and whether they would move over." Continuing to develop and offer a boxed product meant some significant portion of customers would never shift to a subscription.

With this announcement, Adobe signaled that it was wholly and completely committing itself to a box-free, cloud-based world. There was no going back. "What was important is that we could look any customer in the eye and say, 'You are better off under this new subscription offering and this new paradigm than you were before. And that's why we feel that it's so important for you to move over,'" said Garrett capturing the executives' sentiment at this pivotal time.

Adobe needed every ounce of conviction to stick to this decision. A Change.org petition created by outraged Photoshop customers quickly circulated, garnering over fifty thousand signatures.[51] Detractors believed that the move to Creative Cloud was an attempt by Adobe to extract more revenues from users and wanted nothing to do with it. If Adobe hadn't burned the boats, it would have been tempting to give in and carve out the Photoshop perpetual software product from Creative Cloud.

But with no option to go back available, Adobe sat down with key influencers and customers to listen to their concerns. In response, the company developed a lower-cost subscription offering specifically for photographers, which included just Photoshop and Lightroom for only ten dollars a month versus fifty dollars a month for the entire Creative Cloud offering. Adobe's responsiveness and flexibility to address the needs and concerns of customers quelled the uprising and demonstrated Adobe's commitment to customers even further.

I was closely following Adobe during this period, and what impressed me was how committed and determined the executive team was. A friend who worked at Adobe during this time summarized it well: "The Adobe executives faced huge blowback from customers, employees, and investors during these two years. And they never blinked." That executive solidarity gave Adobe the audacity to declare that declining revenues and profits were a good thing for the company.

Have no doubt: this was a highly disruptive, tumultuous time for Adobe. But a focus on customers, a commitment to transparency, and a willingness to burn the boats allowed the business to come out the other end better and stronger. Adobe's strategy for disruptive growth was different from traditional strategy and change management because it required setting and making a huge bet on the future, something that the organization hadn't done in the past. And it paid off. In 2018, Adobe's revenues were two times what they were in 2012, net income was three and a half times, and the stock price was seven times.

"Do or do not. There is no try."

—Yoda

How to Burn Your Boats

Something stupendous happens when you focus. Your vision narrows, and you see only the one thing that matters. Sounds and distractions fade away, and time slows way down. There is just you and the object of your focus. There is clarity in your purpose. You are all in.

Achieving that focus and commitment is what burning the boats is all about. By eliminating all options for retreat, you can become single-mindedly focused on success and victory. This is why burning your boats is so crucial for a disruption growth strategy: your transformation will be a long, arduous, and exhausting journey and it will be tempting to turn around and go back. Burning your boats will not be easy. As humans, we are conditioned to have options, to have a plan B, because escape routes and backup plans protect us if we don't seem to be achieving our goal.

Burning the boats is all about forcing full commitment when making one is difficult. You'll gather as many data as possible, understand the risk, and use your best judgment to make a decision. And once you make it, you will stick with it. There can be no second-guessing, no "what-ifs." You'll make contingency plans only in anticipation of roadblocks that will come your way, finding ways around the obstacles. But you will always keep moving forward because everything depends on it.

You don't have to be the top person in your organization leading a disruptive transformation to engage in burning your boats; it's a useful exercise for any leader. The following best practices eliminate distractions and help you become wholly committed to the success of your disruptive strategy.

Set a deadline. You probably don't have an actual enemy chasing after you, so you'll need to create one. Set a deadline, ideally one that instills a bit of a panic in you and forces you to hit it. One person bought a first-class nonrefundable ticket to Japan for a product launch.[52] This person knew the product had to be ready for launch or the business would suffer a big penalty. Similar, if you are transitioning from one product to another or shifting from one strategy to the other, set a clear deadline to give everyone just enough time to make adjustments—and then flip the switch. Don't be lulled into thinking there's a perfect time or a right time.

Experience what it feels to be all in. When was the last time you were all in? Recall what it was like to pursue a meaningful goal, the exhilaration of taking each step forward, the exhaustion you felt, but also the elation of tasting sweet success. Give yourself and your team a taste of what it feels like to be all-in with a short sprint project. Done right, you will all be looking forward to more.

Remove dabblers and right-timers. Identify the people who are standing in the way of your organization being all in. Dabblers are people who like to dip their toe in the water, unable to commit to one direction or the other; they like to keep their options open. Right-timers find a way to say, "It's not the perfect time to move. We need XYZ." For them, there will never be a right time to commit. Stay away from them or, better yet, move them out of your team or even the organization. You need people who are ready to be fully committed and all in with the strategy.

Make plan B highly unpalatable. What if retreat wasn't a comfortable option? It may be tempting to hold some of your reserves back to fund a backup plan, but that would mean you're not investing fully in your transformation strategy. Putting it all in means you could retreat—not back to the status quo but to a much worse situation. Who wants that?

Make the call. In the end, you are the only one who can make the call to move forward. Identify your boats, and be prepared to burn them. What's holding you back, keeping you from being all in? Is it fear of failure? Lack of resources or data? As a leader, you've experienced failure and you have survived. But you will never create transformative change and experience exponential growth if you don't make the call.

BETTING YOUR NONPROFIT'S FUTURE ON DISRUPTIVE GROWTH

As you can see from the Adobe example, creating and executing a disruptive transformation that creates exponential growth takes a lot of work. It is not for the faint of heart. I'll give one more example, this time from a nonprofit to illustrate that disruptive growth isn't something that just businesses pursue. Any type of organization can aspire to achieve. And as you'll see, it's just as gut wrenching to make it happen.

When Paul LeBlanc took over as president of Southern New Hampshire University, a nonprofit institution, in 2003, it was a struggling campus in Manchester, New Hampshire, with twenty-five hundred students. The university had a strong sense of mission: historically it served mostly nontraditional students who didn't have many options for higher education and often worked full time and went to school at night or on the weekends. But by 2003, most of the students on the campus were traditional young adults.

As LeBlanc settled into his new role, he became intrigued by the small online learning division tucked into a back corner of the campus as a way to return to the university's roots. "The world equally distributes talent, but it doesn't equally distribute opportunity," he observed.[53] "Paths are not always the same." He could see the potential of the Internet not only to expand education beyond the classroom but also to meet students' needs, which were evolving in response to a rapidly changing world.

LeBlanc was also closely watching for-profit institutions like the University of Phoenix and Kaplan, which were growing quickly. He felt that the timing was perfect for a nonprofit, accredited university like SNHU to take on these giants. A key difference was that SNHU was hyperfocused on student success, specifically on making sure students graduated with an accredited degree without taking on onerous student debt. He recalled telling his board, "We have this small window to do something big."

With the go-ahead from the board, LeBlanc took several years to carefully plan and execute a new online division. Like Adobe, SNHU took its time to get it right. LeBlanc hired top talent from for-profit organizations to bring in their marketing and operational expertise. They decamped the online operations to the converted old clothing mills in downtown Manchester. And they adopted marketing and student recruitment best practices from for-profit organizations. For example, SNHU's research found that students were far more likely to enroll with the first school that responded to their inquiry, so they expanded enrollment staffing to evenings and weekends, which was when most students were researching and applying.

But they also maintained the mission of a nonprofit institution: investing in academic and financial advisers to ensure that students were taking the right courses based on their financial constraints and learning strengths. Very importantly, LeBlanc struck new governance agreements with the on-campus faculty that gave them thirty days to raise concerns about a course being taken online—but they couldn't stop a course from going online. The support of faculty from an accredited university was crucial. LeBlanc wanted to ensure that online students were receiving the same quality education as their on-campus counterparts.

By October 2010, SNHU was ready to go big with a national TV ad campaign. They had ambitions to grow from $50 million to $100 million in revenues and increase by ten times the number of students they served. But that fall, LeBlanc sat at his desk staring at two pieces of paper in front of him. One showed the promising results of a recent ten-week-test TV ad buy in select markets that showed they were generating a lot of leads. But they were just leads. It wasn't clear yet what the conversion rates would be. It was too early to tell.

The other piece of paper showed the growing deficit caused by the university's financial meltdown. Student enrollment had dropped drastically, and for the first time in the university's history, there was a projected $3 million deficit for year end on the $50 million budget— and it was growing.

LeBlanc's dilemma was this: Should they go ahead and invest $2 million as planned for a national TV ad buy to launch the online degree program? It was $2 million of cash that they didn't have to spare. If the anticipated enrollments didn't materialize, he would be jeopardizing SNHU's financial stability and future . But if he delayed the launch, he risked letting the for-profit players widen their lead.

The only data they didn't have was the effectiveness of the ad buy. But LeBlanc had confidence that the team could optimize the execution and hit the planned revenue. "It was a big gulp moment for us," he remembered. "There was a sense that this was the time. Now or never." This was their burn-the-boats moment: they committed to the TV ad buy. Now they had to hope it would work.

The results were astounding. SNHU saw its enrollment rate double overnight, and it continued to accelerate. LeBlanc came back to the board in January 2011 to ask for another $4 million to expand the national TV ad buy, and it was given without question. Today, SNHU has 102,000 degree-seeking students and another 40,000 students seeking credentials or certifications. The student graduation rate is 50 percent versus percentages in the low to mid 20's for comparable colleges.[54] Revenues reached $850 million in 2018 with profits of $102 million, a 12 percent margin, that it can reinvest into expanding programs and access.

SNHU continues to drive disruptive transformation. It plans to hit $1 billion in revenue in 2020, and its stated goal to is serve 300,000 students by 2022. It works with the Institute for the Future to identify and understand who its students will be in 2030. They are developing competency-based education, with the goal of reducing tuition cost to $100 a month (yes, that's right: less than $2,000 a year in tuition!) to make a college education affordable to anyone who wants one. And SNHU is spearheading initiatives to enable refugees in countries like Kenya, Lebanon, Malawi, and South Africa to earn a US-accredited degree by using technology and project-based learning.[55]

I love the SNHU example because it exemplifies all of the things that a disruptive transformation organization does well: a singular focus on the needs of future students, the courage to make a big gulp decision with insufficient data, and the stirring success of resulting exponential growth. It shows that big breakthrough ideas can come from anywhere, even a small, hitherto unknown university. The world has so many problems that need to be addressed that the only way we can hope to tackle them is to drive exponential change and growth in solutions.

MOVING FORWARD

Conventional wisdom is that organizations cannot disrupt themselves—that there are too many entrenched interests to dismantle, that too radical a transformation would tear an organization apart. But Adobe and SNHU prove otherwise. At any point they could have turned back from the brink, seeing the daunting challenges ahead as insurmountable. But they persisted, finding a deep conviction to keep moving forward—a conviction that came from that clear vision of who they were trying to serve.

As you move forward with your disruptive transformation planning, keep coming back to whom you are trying to serve, framing your "why," your purpose around the needs of your future customers. Practice transparency to build accountability and trust that will carry you through the tough times. And most important, make it clear that the only option is to push forward so that you win the full commitment of your team to execute the strategy.

TAKEAWAYS

- Plan on spending a lot of time and resources to conduct rigorous research and help build the case for your disruption strategy.
- Build and maintain trust with transparency. To get buy-in, you need people to believe that you are committed to listening to and sharing with them—-and to shifting the strategy as needed.
- Secure the full commitment of your team or organization by figuratively burning the boats. Everyone must be all in and understand retreat is not an option.

"It's only a movement if it moves without you."

—Jeremy Heimans and Henry Timms, Co-authors of *New Power*

CHAPTER 3
· · · · · · · · · · ·
LEADING A
DISRUPTIVE MOVEMENT

───────────●───────────

HAVE YOU ever been part of a movement? Attended a sport, religious, or political rally? Marched for social justice or fundraised for a cause? Then you know what it's like to believe in and belong to a movement that seeks to change the status quo.

A movement is simply a group of people working together to achieve a particular set of goals. In movements, the vision and purpose develop a life of their own, moving beyond the influence of a single leader, to be taken up by those who want to be a part of the change.

In my research, I found leaders who deliberately started movements to create disruptive transformation. To drive disruptive growth, everyone affected by the growth strategy must understand it and how they play a part in it. They must also be inspired to believe that together, they would achieve things they once thought were impossible.

Movements help leaders do two things. First, they draw others into the transformation. To execute an audacious growth strategy, every person in the organization must be inspired to take coordinated, intentional action. There is no room for passive participants on the sidelines, awaiting orders in a disruptive transformation. You need every person contributing and leading from where they stand. In that way, a movement catches fire and spreads, taking on a life of its own and no longer constrained by the limits of anyone's influence.

Second, movements create a strong sense of tribalism and belonging that binds and carries people through the tough times. When people are faced with a setback or uncertainty, being part of a movement reminds them that they are not alone, that together they can all overcome this challenge.

In 2010, I wrote *Open Leadership*, which explains how leaders can be more open, transparent, and authentic in order to build better relationships with the people they aspire to lead. My surprising finding was that leaders need *more* rigor and discipline to be open than to be closed and shut off. You have to define how open, how transparent, how authentic you will be. It's the same with movements: as you prepare to let go so that a movement can flourish, you must spend more time defining its parameters. You need to set guidelines and standards while also decentralizing and democratizing decision making. You need to create unity around a central statement of purpose while also providing space for a babel of voices to emerge. And you need to remind everyone about the common vision, inspiring them to remain engaged and active rather than controlling and directing their every action.

Let's turn our attention to a leader who did just that—and his cause grew faster than anyone would have ever imagined.

MOVEMENTS AREN'T CONTROLLED; THEY ARE INSPIRED

The hardest part about driving a disruptive growth strategy is that you have to set up just enough structure to guide and inspire a movement within your organization—and then you have to let go. Disruptive leaders recognize that movements aren't controlled; they are inspired. When people are inspired, they make the movement their personal mission, going the extra mile, moving a lot faster, and driving growth exponentially.

One recent fall evening in San Francisco, I had a chance to see the fruit of this approach at a gala fundraiser for Sponsors for Educational Opportunity (SEO), a nonprofit that prepares underserved, underrepresented young people for success in college and in their careers. The high school students whom SEO works with come from households with average incomes of less than $32,000 a year, a demographic group that typically sees only 20 percent of high school graduates going on to college. But at SEO, 100 percent of the students go on to college and 90 percent of them graduate thanks to the continued college mentoring program that SEO provides.

The ballroom that evening was packed with more than three hundred of the top movers and shakers of the city, assembled to hear from luminaries like Henry Kravis, co-CEO of KKR, one of the largest investment firms in the world; Dan Schulman, CEO of PayPal; and Vicky Tsai, founder of the beauty brand Tatcha and herself a graduate of SEO.

While they were all impressive speakers, the most captivating speaker of the evening was Enrique, a senior high school student who lives in a studio apartment with his parents, brother and grandmother. Enrique almost didn't get up on the stage that evening, but he was determined to share his struggles and his dreams. He was humble, he was funny, and he represented the human potential that SEO seeks to propel. As Enrique sat down, the Fund-a-Need donation portion of the evening immediately followed, raising $350,000 of the total $1.4 million raised that evening.

But SEO is far more than a heartwarming story. It's an example of an organization that had to disrupt and transform itself to become what it is today. Annually, SEO supports almost a thousand high school students and 850 college students in the United States, Beijing, Shanghai, Hong Kong, Ho Chih Minh City, Hanoi, Lagos, and Accra (the capital of Ghana). But for almost twenty years before that, it was a small, struggling program in New York City.

Its founder, Michael Osheowitz, came of age in the civil rights era. While he was building a career on Wall Street, eventually becoming president of the financial consulting firm Arthur Schmidt & Associates, he founded Sponsors for Educational Opportunity (SEO) in New York City in 1963. The goal of the organization was to mentor underserved students to help them gain admission to competitive colleges and universities. As an investment banker, he had a network of people at banks and accounting firms whom he could tap to become mentors.

By the late 1970s, SEO had helped hundreds of students of color complete high school and go on to college, but it was struggling to recruit both students and mentors. Mentorship quality varied highly depending on mentors' abilities to help students very different from themselves. These mentors also couldn't provide what was needed to supplement New York City's deteriorating academic programs. Osheowitz had also counted on graduating SEO students to come back and serve as mentors themselves, but few did, meaning that SEO had to constantly recruit mentors.

To keep SEO going, Osheowitz realized that SEO needed to formalize its programs with hired staff who could create and deliver a rich curriculum to prepare students for the rigors of college. At the same time, he had always harbored a dream to diversify the financial industry. He believed that SEO could be a catalyst to change the face of Wall Street. The problem was that the financial industry was behind other industries in diversifying their workforce. Unlike many other Fortune 500 companies, most investment banks did not have formal programs to identify and hire people of color at the time.

Osheowitz realized that if he could make SEO relevant to investment banking, he could do three things at the same time: (1) diversify banking, (2) create opportunities to expose talented young people to a career they had never contemplated pursuing, and (3) secure the financial support of the investment banking industry for all of SEO's programs.

In late 1979, Osheowitz was introduced by Robert Menschel, a senior director at Goldman Sachs, to John Whitehead, then cochairman of Goldman Sachs, the largest and preeminent investment bank on Wall Street. Osheowitz's financial consulting firm had worked with Whitehead on several deals, so the two knew each other well. Whitehead was also familiar with SEO because Osheowitz talked about the program all the time with anyone that he knew. "We started talking about how white and how male dominated the investment banking industry was," Osheowitz recalls. "I told John that I thought that we, SEO, could actually do something about that, and would he help me?"

Whitehead quickly embraced the idea and asked Osheowitz, Robert Menschel, and HR director Robert Burke, to develop the plan. Once the plan was in place, Whitehead connected Osheowitz with Robert Baldwin, chairman of Morgan Stanley, and George Shinn, chairman of First Boston. Introductions to CEOs of other Wall Street firms quickly followed.

The idea was simple and compelling: SEO would identify the most talented college students of color in the United States for paid internships at the participating investment banking firms during the summer after their junior year of college. At the start of the summer, SEO would provide a "boot camp" to go over the formal and unwritten rules of Wall Street. The CEOs and other senior partners at those firms would provide seminars throughout the summer and assign a mentor from the firm to guide each student during the summer.

In the depth of the winter in 1980, Osheowitz visited top colleges and universities holding information sessions. More than one hundred students of color applied, and SEO selected eleven students—four women and seven men from Harvard, Yale, Columbia, Dartmouth, and Wesleyan—to make up the first class. There was tremendous pressure placed on them. An early participant and later SEO board chair Walter Booker remembers, "It was made clear to us that we weren't just in this for ourselves. … If you messed up, you weren't just hurting yourself, but closing off an opportunity at that company for those who would come after you."[56] Not only did no one mess up; they all excelled. At the end of the summer, all eleven interns were offered full-time jobs at the firms where they had interned.

Today, the investment banking program is part of SEO Careers and includes internships and mentoring in other fields such as law, corporate management, and management consulting. More than 75 percent of its more than fourteen thousand graduates have received full-time job offers from major financial services firms. The program now includes internship and mentoring programs in other industries too, such as management consulting and alternative investments. Moreover, the financial support from investment banks allowed the high school program to expand, with more than thirteen thousand alumni having graduated from college.

What began as one person's dream has become a movement. I've seen its impact firsthand. As a result of my research into SEO, I became a mentor to a high school junior in San Francisco. Over half of my fellow mentors are themselves SEO alumni. After forty years of involvement, many of the early participants now sit in the executive ranks of America's top companies, contributing much-needed gender and ethnic diversification.

Michael Osheowitz's success in kicking SEO into high-growth mode in 1980 was predicated on one key insight: his realization that he couldn't be the leader of the movement. Indeed, his humility and self-deprecation stand out as an anomaly in the financial services industry. He admits that being out in front did not suit his personality.

More important, he realized that for SEO to grow, he had to step aside and allow others to build the movement as if it was their own. "To accomplish things in an important way, you have to make others truly believe that they are ones who are creating the change, and support them and step back, and be willing to not be in the limelight," he told me. The CEOs of Wall Street's top financial institutions needed to make the program their own. Such was the case with Henry Kravis, the founder and CEO of the private equity firm KKR. Kravis was one of the founders of SEO's Alternative Investing Program and as he got to know SEO, the more convinced he became of SEO's opportunities. He became Chairman of SEO in 2014 and, along with SEO president William Goodloe, has been responsible for driving SEO's recent growth and results.

For many leaders, giving up control is one of the major reasons they shy away from movement making: it feels too risky and dangerous to let others play a leadership role during tumultuous, disruptive times. I understand how uncomfortable that can be, but I also know firsthand that letting go pays off.

> # "Never doubt that a small group of thoughtful, committed citizens can change the world. Indeed, it's the only thing that ever has."
>
> —Attributed to Margaret Mead, cultural anthropologist

In the early days of Altimeter, I brought on three other partners capable of driving our strategy and presence in exponential ways. I had to be willing to give up control and embrace them as equal partners. The result was they were each willing to put their personal brands and followers behind the Altimeter brand. Altimeter's brand and influence grew very quickly, rivaling established analyst firms many times bigger than we were. Our combined strength was greater than what we could muster as individuals.

The key to be able to let go and let others take over the movement is to recruit the right followers. Let's take a closer look at how to find and develop those crucial first followers.

FINDING YOUR FIRST FOLLOWERS

To create a disruptive transformation movement, you need followers—and not just any followers, but people who will step up, lead, and embrace the movement as if it is their own. In 1988, Robert Kelley published one of the first academic pieces on followership, "In Praise of Followers," in *Harvard Business Review*. In that piece, he identifies five main types of followers in organizations (see Figure 3.1).[57]

Most employees are dependent and uncritical, falling into two categories of what Kelley called "Sheep" (passive and uncritical, lacking in initiative and sense of responsibility) and "Yes People" (actively deferential, dependent on a leader for inspiration). Those in another category of followers, "Alienated," are critical and independent thinkers but passive in their roles; something happened along the way that turned them into disgruntled cynics. "Survivors" don't fall into a formal category of followers; they are people who are able to morph into any of the other four types of followers depending on who is leading them.

But if you want your disruptive growth strategy to succeed, you are going to have to find, develop, and fill your organization with what Kelley called "Effective Followers"— people who "think for themselves and carry out their duties and assignments with energy and assertiveness … they are risk takers, self-starters, and independent problem solvers." As Kelley points out, these are the same qualities of an effective leader. "Followership is not a person but a role," he writes, "and what distinguishes followers from leaders is not intelligence or character but the role they play."

How can you find and develop these effective followers? By intentionally defining and nurturing a relationship between you and your followers. As leadership gurus Jim Kouzes and Barry Posner explain in their seminal book, *The Leadership Challenge*, "Leadership is a relationship between those who aspire to lead and those who are inspired to follow."[58] As a leader, you set expectations of what it

Fig. 3.1 Five Types of Followers

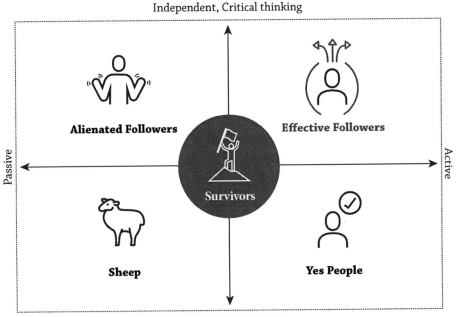

Independent, Critical thinking

Alienated Followers

Effective Followers

Passive

Active

Survivors

Sheep

Yes People

Dependent, Uncritical thinking

Source: Robert Kelley, *Harvard Business Review* (November 1988)

means to be an effective follower and also define followers' roles and responsibilities in relation to the leader: you. Will they blindly follow your orders? Or will they put on the mantle of leadership themselves?

Practicing and defining followership is especially important in building a disruptive movement because things are moving and changing so quickly that you need effective followers who can step into leadership roles. And as we saw with Michael Osheowitz and SEO, the most important followers you must secure are your first followers. Goldman Sachs CEO John Whitehead quickly morphed into the role of being a leader, recruiting other first followers to SEO.

In a TED Talk "How to Start a Movement," Derek Sivers illustrates the importance of first followers very well.[59] In the talk, he shows a video of a shirtless guy on a hillside dancing to some unheard music. Here are transcript highlights:

A leader needs the guts to stand alone and look ridiculous. What he's doing is so easy to follow. Here's his first follower with a crucial role; he's going to show everyone else how to follow.

Notice that the leader embraces him as an equal. Now it's not about the leader anymore; it's about them, plural. It takes guts to stand out like that. The first follower transforms a lone nut into a leader. And here comes a second follower. Now it's not a lone nut, it's not two nuts—three is a crowd and a crowd is news. A movement must be public. It's important to show not just the leader, but the followers, because you find that new followers emulate the followers, not the leader.

Here come two more people, and immediately after, three more people. Now we've got momentum. This is the tipping point. Now we've got a movement. As more people join in, it's less risky. So those that were sitting on the fence before now have no reason not to. They won't stand out. They won't be ridiculed but they will be part of the in-crowd if they hurry.

There are two takeaways from this TED Talk. First, the leader embraces the first follower as an equal. Second, the first follower validates the leader, confirming that the vision isn't crazy. This is what happened between Michael Osheowitz and John Whitehead: the credibility of Whitehead as the first follower kick-started the movement that would drive SEO's disruptive growth.

You may not be able to secure the followership of the CEO of the most prestigious investment bank in the world for your disruptive transformation strategy. You may not even get many members of your executive team to listen to your ideas. But all you need is one first follower to be inspired by what you want to accomplish and enable that person to bring on more followers.

Employees (and customers) will buy into your disruptive strategy only if you have credibility and they trust you. And they will become ardent followers and part of a movement only if they believe you have their best interests at the core of everything you do. In his professional life, Osheowitz had developed a deep network throughout the investment banking world, and they all knew that he was passionate about SEO, so he walked into the initial discussions about the expansion of SEO with credibility. But he had to earn their trust by engaging with them as full and equal partners.

THREE WAYS TO BUILD YOUR MOVEMENT

Much like Osheowitz understood that he needed to spark a movement among Wall Street leaders to grow SEO and diversify Wall Street, T-Mobile's CEO, John Legere, knew that he needed to make the Un-carrier strategy I write about in Chapter 1 a movement, especially within T-Mobile. The Un-carrier strategy was centered on the company as a customer advocate. But Legere understood that *saying* the business was going to be a customer advocate wasn't going to be enough. To be truly different, to really be the Un-carrier. T-Mobile and everyone at it had to *be* a customer advocate in everything that they did, and in the process create a movement that energized employees and customers. Legere's logic was that if T-Mobile was going to listen to customers and then do what customers said they wanted, the company had to change how it approached everything.

In terms of style, you probably couldn't find leaders who were more different than Michael Osheowitz and John Legere: Osheowitz stays out of the spotlight, whereas Legere relishes public engagement. The way they show up and develop relationships stems from the type of person, and thus leader, that both are. But there's no doubt that creating a movement is at the center of the leadership practice of both men.

Many of you are likely sitting at a fork in the road, deciding if and how you will pursue a disruptive growth strategy. It's critical that you think through how you will show up as a leader. How will you—like Osheowitz and Legere—intentionally create and sustain a movement that can make your disruptive growth a reality?

In my research, I've found that there are three ways to build a movement:

1. Identify followers and define your relationship with them.

2. Write a manifesto that inspires action.

3. Sustain a consistent leadership presence.

I'll show you *why* they work and *how* they worked, especially at T-Mobile—and provide advice on how you can start executing them.

IDENTIFY FOLLOWERS AND DEFINE YOUR RELATIONSHIP WITH THEM

As T-Mobile developed its Un-carrier strategy, the company knew that if it was going to listen to customers and then do what they said they wanted, then T-Mobile employees would have to approach doing their jobs in a new way. Legere realized that he needed to connect with employees and define what the relationship would be like.

One pre-launch moment was particularly important to creating momentum internally with employees. In fall 2012, Legere saw the upcoming Consumer Electronics Show (CES) as an opportunity to preview the Un-carrier positioning. At that point, T-Mobile had nothing significant to announce, but Legere nevertheless took the opportunity to make head-turning pronouncements. Here's an excerpt of what he said onstage at the T-Mobile press conference:[60]

Our network is faster than AT&T and Verizon in New York City. Anybody here from New York? Anybody here use AT&T? Any of you that use it, are you happy? Of course not, because the network's crap!

I think you can see us going into first quarter as we start some of these specific Un-carrier messages going right at it with attitude. I think you'll see some swagger, you'll see some attitude, you'll see some aggressive attacks on our competition. All in fun of course....

It's going to be about solving customers' pain points. Customers that can't stand opaque billing, lack of transparency, surprises, being locked in, lack of flexibility, lack of ability to control their own destiny and their being treated like second class citizens because of their length and term of service.

This is not the way that a CEO usually talks! Legere was taking on the competition head-on, calling them "crap" and implying that they were lying. "John just talked completely differently and showed up completely differently from any other telco executive," Andrew Sherrard, the senior vice president of marketing at T-Mobile at the time, recalled.

While the CES appearance made a splash with press, Legere knew who his more important audience was: the employees back home watching. Imagine that you are a weary T-Mobile employee and you just saw your CEO stand up onstage and publicly and aggressively challenge the industry leader. The employees, driving hard to make the Un-carrier launch in March happen, could see that Legere was out there standing up for them, taking the fight to the competitors. "That helped rally the company," Sherrard remembered. "When John said that, it only accelerated [our efforts]."

As a leader, Legere understood that the journey ahead was going to be long and exhausting, stretching into years. He had to rally the

T-Mobile organization to do more than execute on the strategy; his employees had to believe that everyone was on a crusade to change the mobile landscape on behalf of their customers. He recognized them and treated them as his first followers.

How to Keep Follower Relationships at the Center of Your Movement

To build a movement the way Legere did, you need to think carefully about how to engage your followers. Imagine that a year from now, you are holding a meeting with those most involved in your movement. Who is in the room? Who's running the meeting? How are decisions made? How much are you talking during that meeting? There are no right or wrong answers to these questions, but taking the time to consider them will help you define what the relationship will be among you, the first followers, and the movement. To help you get there, consider these two best practices:

Identify your first followers. You need only one or two people to get started, but don't jump at the first person who raises a hand! Michael Osheowitz waited for decades for the right time and the right person to show up before starting the investment banking program at SEO. He knew that without that key first follower, he had little chance of successfully launching the program. John Legere painted the landscape more broadly, speaking to the internal audience of T-Mobile employees, especially those working on the Un-carrier initiative. Take a moment to define who your ideal first follower would be—not so much in terms of a specific person, but the capabilities and resources that person or persons would bring to kick-start the movement. It could be connections, but it may also be a willingness to roll up their sleeves and get to work.

Define the relationship from the follower point of view. As a leader, it's tempting to define and measure the relationship from your or the organization's point of view. But step back and look at it from the followers' perspective. What's in it for them? Here are a few more questions to guide your thinking process on this issue:

How will followers feel about their relationship with you a year from now? Dig deep into how you think they would feel after a discussion with you. I hope that words like empowered, energized, trusted, motivated, and inspired will be on that list. What do you need to do as a leader to create a relationship that will foster these feelings?

How will information be shared and decisions made to create those feelings you just defined? Trust and relationships don't develop in a vacuum; they are built with each successful interaction between people. What information can you share early on to indicate that you not only trust your followers, but believe they can use and act on that knowledge? What questions and decisions will you come to them with to show that you not only value their input but are also confident that they can make the decision on their own?

What are your strengths and shortcomings—and are you willing to share them? Nothing builds trust and relationships faster than honesty and vulnerability. Your first followers will want to know where you feel you can best contribute and also where they can fill in a weakness or shortcoming you have. This is not to say that you have to share everything about yourself with them, but ask yourself what you can share to build and deepen the relationship.

WRITE A MANIFESTO THAT INSPIRES ACTION

Once you've defined your relationship with your followers, it's critical that you inspire them to remain engaged and active in your movement and disruptive growth strategy. You must remind them of your common purpose so they can act independently. At the same time, you must provide them parameters so everyone acts in unison. Most companies have a vision statement that they hope will be that north star for their employees. A vision statement is a single sentence (usually) that serves as a shorthand way to capture where you want to be in the future. The problem is that a single sentence leaves much to interpretation.

That's why manifestos are so important to a disruptive growth strategy: they paint a picture of the future in bold, vivid details. A manifesto is a public declaration of the objective and intentions of the organization. It is written with future customers in mind, telling them why you exist and documenting what your organization believes in. The manifesto also attracts people—employees and customers—who want to be part of your movement.

There have been some notable manifestos throughout history. Martin Luther nailed his 95 Theses to the door of the Wittenberg Castle Church in 1517—and started the Protestant Reformation.[61] The Communist Manifesto written by Karl Marx and Friedrich Engels in 1848 served as the justification for communist revolutions around the world.[62] Today organizations of all kinds use manifestos. Here are a few examples, and their full text along with the T-Mobile Manifesto are available in the Appendix:

- Apple. The company's 2011 "Think Different" ad campaign is essentially a manifesto. It begins, "Here's to the crazy ones…"
- Nextdoor. A neighborhood-based social network, Nextdoor begins its manifesto with the words, "We are for neighbors."
- (Red). The last line of the manifesto of this nonprofit created to rid the world of AIDS reads, "There is an end to AIDS. It's you."
- Piedmont Health. The Atlanta-based health care provider created

the manifesto to bring its experience principles to life for employees, with the words, "to make a difference in every life we touch."

T-Mobile joined the ranks of these organizations to create a powerful manifesto ahead of the March 2013 Un-carrier launch. At that time, T-Mobile had 40,000 employees who not only needed to understand the Un-carrier strategy, but also had to change almost everything that they said and did at work to become the embodiment of the Un-carrier to customers. It was a huge amount of change to create in a very short time.

Initially created as a marketing communication guide, the Un-carrier Manifesto (see Figure 3.2) got traction internally as a guide for product and experience development.[63] From there it moved into frontline employee activation, from the call centers to retail storefronts, to bring the Un-carrier strategy to life. The first and last paragraphs of the manifesto capture the vision and actions needed to become the Un-carrier: "We're in the changing the phone-company business" and "We will be un-relenting."

T-Mobile also changed the way it trained employees—the people who would be creating the Un-carrier experience for customers. Since T-Mobile was launching changes so quickly, there were inevitably times when things did not go as plan. Education and training included scenarios where standard policies and procedures could be broken, empowering employers to treat each customer as an individual. In those moments, with no script or procedure set in place, employees had to rely on their recall of the Un-carrier Manifesto to guide their actions.

I tested this in a recent visit to a T-Mobile store at a local mall, when I asked two sales reps how their bonus compensation worked. They said that half of their individual bonus was based on how much they each sold to customers. The other half was based on the customer satisfaction score for the entire store. They all had to work together as a team to make sure that customers were listened to and served. Each went into great detail about how this worked, giving examples of how they would take care each other's customers *because that's what they did as the Un-carrier.*

HOW TO CRAFT A MANIFESTO THAT RESULTS IN ACTION

To create your own manifesto, think of it as the broad strokes of a narrative for your movement. If your employees and customers are going to follow you on the tough, risky disruptive transformation journey ahead, it's not enough for them to understand the manifesto. They have to *feel* it, remember it, and make it their own. They may not remember it verbatim, but they will recall the emotion and tap into it to guide the specific actions they come up with on their own.

Here are some tips to help you start writing your manifesto:

Start with a rant. In a great post, business writer Shannon Tanton recommends taking this approach: Identify what's wrong with the world.[64] How would things be so much better if only people did something differently? If you had a magic wand, what would you change about your industry? Take all of the things you don't like about how things are today and put them down in writing. I guarantee you that it will be fun and you will feel great.

Flip the rant into a belief. Turn each negative rant into a positive statement. For example, here's a simple rant: "As a former dog-lover-turned-cat-owner, I think it's shameful that cats are treated as second-class pets." I then flip it into a belief: "Cats deserve first-class treatment because we love them with all of our heart."

Add what you are going to do to act on that belief. A manifesto is a playbook that lays out how those beliefs will "manifest" in the real world. Follow this simple template, "We believe [that something is true] and that's why we will [do something]." With my cat example, if I were a veterinarian clinic, my manifesto would be, "Because we love our cats, we believe they deserve first-class treatment and parity of care. That's why we have a dedicated waiting and exam room for them, away from barking dogs and their scents."

After you write a few manifesto statements, whittle them down and strengthen them by following these best practices:

Use a collective and active voice. The collective voice gives the manifesto a call to action and a promise of belonging, beckoning, "Are you with us?" The active voice sets expectations of action and engagement. Nextdoor, the neighborhood-based social network, has a manifesto that makes frequent use of strong terms like, "We believe," "We embrace," "We choose."

Write a blog post about each statement. If the statement were the title of a blog post, would there be enough content and meaning there to write a few paragraphs? If a statement truly lays out a foundational belief, you should have plenty to say about it. If you can't write a paragraph or two about the statement, you shouldn't include it in your manifesto.

Test with customers. After you've winnowed your statements down, show your manifesto to a few customers, or even do some substantive customer testing. Do the statements resonate with them? Do they feel differently about your organization after reading it? Do they believe that something will be different because of what you do? Test and refine your statements with and for your customers. After all, it's all about them.

Keep it to a page. Make your manifesto compact enough to fit on a page so that you can make it into a poster for your office, post it on Instagram in a readable format, or save it as a desktop image. The intent here is to share and spread your manifesto, putting it in places where it strategically reminds customers and employees about your view of the future. If it stretches into pages, no one is going to read it.

Once you have a manifesto that you love, be sure to share it widely. After all, have you ever seen a quiet movement? If you have a movement worth following, you will find every possible opportunity to get your manifesto in front of your existing and potential followers.

Let's now turn to the third and final leg of building a movement: the role of the leader in the movement.

SUSTAIN A CONSISTENT LEADERSHIP PRESENCE

As leaders, we've been told to be humble, to be a servant leader, to put our organizations ahead of ourselves. The problem is that we've confused being humble and prioritizing the company with not being visible—that is, not being out there reminding people of your shared purpose and vision. People get busy. That's why it's important to remind them over and over again the *why* of what you are all doing. Because if you don't do, who will?

That's why if you are leading a disruptive growth strategy, you must maintain a consistent leadership presence.

I recently spoke at a Fortune 500 company's internal marketing training session, and we ended the day with a question-and-answer session with the chief marketing officer. I asked her what the marketing objectives were for the year, and she proudly turned to her team and said, "Ask them. We developed it together." An embarrassed, awkward silence followed. Not a single person in the entire department could recount the five key parts of the strategy. She admitted afterward that she had wrongly assumed that because they had worked long and hard on the strategy together, the team had internalized it. The reality is that day-to-day priorities pushed those objectives out of sight and out of mind.

You must be constant and consistent in your support of the movement. And for you to do that, you must be comfortable being an open leader. Being open doesn't mean that you share everything about yourself. As one leader said, pointing to the number of leaders posting food photos on Instagram, "Who cares what I had for lunch?" I heartily agree. I don't care about what you had for lunch. What I care about is what you talked about over lunch, how you think we are doing, what we should be doing better. I care about what's on your mind, what you are focused on. That's because I'm on the same journey as you. We're in this movement together, and I want to know that you are walking alongside me as we overcome the obstacles in the way.

Michael Osheowitz talked about SEO and the kids whose lives it improved to anyone who cared to listen to him. That's how he launched the movement that transformed the organization into what it is today. But just talking about your movement is no longer enough. You must be visible *and* open on digital. This is not optional. In our fast-changing, distributed world, you *must* use these tools. T-Mobile's Legere understood this right away.

T-Mobile is blessed to have a CEO willing to become the walking embodiment of a customer advocate. When he joined T-Mobile, he looked pretty much like any other CEO: clean-cut, suit, tie. His introductory video message to employees in September 2012, delivered in a no-nonsense manner in a white shirt, was classic tech CEO.[65] But as the Un-carrier strategy took shape, Legere become the public persona of the movement. Now his wardrobe is entirely magenta and black, and he sports long hair (see Figure 3.3).[66]

From the start of his tenure, Legere championed listening to customers. He visited call centers to talk with employees and sit in on their calls with customers. He had a line installed in his office so that he could easily listen in on customer service calls at any time. But more important, he quickly learned to harness social media platforms to drive the movement internally and externally.

It was shortly after the Un-carrier strategy was launched that Legere tried out Twitter (at the suggestion of his daughter) as a way to have direct contact with customers. He didn't tell anyone at T-Mobile that he was doing this. In fact, the security department alerted Legere that someone was impersonating him on Twitter.[67]

Fig. 3.3 The Transformation of T-Mobile CEO John Legere

Getty Images / AP.

Legere uses his Twitter presence to constantly promote T-Mobile, bash competitors, and listen to and respond to customers. He replies constantly to people who mention him on Twitter. The replies are clearly from Legere himself and show a cheeky responsiveness to the people who write to him. The T-Mobile social media team is typically standing by and ready to jump in to help. And never far from Legere's tweeting thumbs are T-Mobile employees who are just as likely to engage with their top executive on Twitter. Legere typically posts and replies to people thirty to fifty times on Twitter alone every day (I counted). By his own admission, Legere spends an inordinate amount of time on social media, sometimes six to seven hours a day.[68]

Why does he do this? Because he's leading by example: showing what it means to be customer obsessed and on a mission to convert everyone into a T-Mobile subscriber because he believes the organization better for them. Legere understood early on the power of digital platforms to create a movement and connect directly with his followers—customers and employees—in an authentic, transparent way. And he was in the right place with the right brand and the right customers and employees who were ready for a new type of relationship with a company.

There are many people who can't stand John Legere, who consider him a showboat and a hack. He doesn't care what they think. For Legere, the people who matter are those he can win over to the Un-carrier and his employees. He constantly highlights the hard-working, hard-charging employees at T-Mobile. He chronicles his frequent visits to call centers and retail stores, which involve a lot of cheering employees, magenta boas, and confetti cannons. These exploits could be seen as one-off back-clapping, but Legere supports them with a consistent presence online, cheering and highlighting his employees over Twitter.

In the end, Legere's fans consider him one of them—someone who's in the trenches fighting for them. And he has many, many fans. As of April 6, 2019, Leger had 6.21 million Twitter followers, which is more than the 4.1 million Twitter followers of AT&T, Verizon, T-Mobile, and Sprint *combined*.[69] That's not a typo: Legere has over 2 million more Twitter followers than all of the top four mobile carriers have combined.

Legere's ability to single-handedly drive engagement with customers and prospects is a key part of the T-Mobile Un-carrier strategy. He's since expanded into a weekly cooking show on Facebook Live, *Slow Cooker Sunday*.[70] It lasts only about fifteen minutes, and Legere (bedecked in a magenta "T-Mobile CEO" apron and chef hat) spends about half the time cooking and the other half pitching T-Mobile. His viewership is now over 3 million people, which is on the same level as prime-time viewership on cable networks.

What's the marketing value of 3 million people watching a weekly show or 6 million Twitter followers? Clearly, John Legere believes in that value and spends far more hours than any other CEO I know of in cultivating a relationship with customers and employees to drive the Un-carrier movement.

The entire leadership at T-Mobile, from the C-suite to the board, understood from the start that a movement was crucial to its disruptive growth strategy. They also understood that their competitors could not do this. While AT&T, Sprint, and Verizon all soon followed with similar business moves—doing away with contracts, offering unlimited data, and so on—they could not mimic or match T-Mobile's movement-building efforts. And most certainly, the CEOs of the companies could not begin to emulate Legere's social media presence and tone, although a few certainly tried.[71]

How to Sustain a Consistent Leadership Presence

There are two steps to leading and sustaining a movement. The first is getting comfortable with being visible and leveraging the many digital and social technologies that are at your disposal. The second is to be constant and consistent in feeding your movement.

In *The Engaged Leader*, I lay out how to be a visible leader in the digital era in great detail. To summarize, there are three things you can do: listen, share, and engage. These are classic leadership actions, but they show up very differently in the digital space and leaders need to be prepared.

Listen to customers and employees. Listening is the way leaders determine what individuals need from them to develop their relationship and deepen their connection. With digital and social tools, you can listen directly and in real-time to customers and employees with no intermediaries. Moreover, you can listen to them at scale by data analytics to surface the most relevant and influential items.

Share your hopes and fears. Sharing is how leaders use stories and other tools to develop mutual understanding and shape the mindsets and actions people take. Digital channels removed much of the friction in sharing, which used to be limited and highly scripted. And yet leaders still treat a tweet or post like a full-fledged press release.

Engage with your followers directly. Engagement is a two-way dialogue that motivates and mobilizes followers to act in concert toward a common purpose. It's also unscripted and open-ended, so leaders don't know where the conversation is going to end when they start.

The second step to focus on is being constant and consistent in your support of the movement. If I were to walk up to one of your frontline employees, would she be able to articulate your strategy? Would she understand how she supports and aligns with it? Would she even care? In many ways, this is the hardest part of creating a movement: sustaining it. Given your disruptive transformation strategy, you are likely going to have to keep feeding and inspiring the movement for the next several years. Here are some best practices on how to do this:

Keep it simple. Don't make it a five-point missive. Create a tagline or use an acronym that serves as a simple reminder of the *why* behind the strategy.

Get over your self-consciousness. It will feel very strange having to repeat yourself over and over again. You'll be thinking, *Aren't they sick of hearing me say this yet again?!?* Watch your audience each time. If you see even one person doing a head nod, ignore all of the people doing eye rolls and keep doing it.

Make repetition a habit. Find appropriate times to engage—at the start of meetings or posting an update at specific time of day, for example.

Mix it up. If the only thing you do is say your mission statement over and over again, you will cringe at yourself. Share new stories that show the impact of the strategy. Try out new channels (take a photo, do a Facebook Live interview) to reach new audiences. A general rule is that if you are getting comfortable, it's probably time to try something new for yourself and your followers.

Be patient. Especially at the start, you will feel as if you are talking into a void. You'll feel like shouting, "Is anyone there?" or "Does anyone care?" My advice: Stick with it while also trying new things. You never know what will resonate with your followers, and almost without fail, if you find something that works, it will be good only for a short while.

MOVING FORWARD

At this point you may have a soundtrack playing in your head that leading a movement is not something you could ever see yourself doing. Keep in mind that I've given you two very different models of movement leaders in this chapter: Michael Osheowitz and John Legere, who are almost polar opposites in terms of personality and approach. Although Osheowitz is not as publicly visible as Legere, his nonstop, passionate advocacy for SEO is the reason the organization is thriving.

While your style and approach may vary, there is one nonnegotiable part of leading the movement: it needs someone to be the spark. So why not you? There is so much opportunity out there, so many problems to be solved, so much work to be done. The only we'll be able to tackle it as organizations and as a society is if brave, passionate leaders like you step forward and create a movement worth believing in.

TAKEAWAYS

- In disruptive times, your leadership needs to shift to create a movement that will sustain your organization as it goes through the long, difficult disruptive transformation.
- Movements require a different kind of leadership where the emphasis is on inspiring followers to take on the mantle of leadership themselves.
- There are three best practices to create and sustain a movement:
    - Identify followers and define your relationship with them.
    - Develop a manifesto that inspires action.
    - Sustain a consistent leadership presence.

"It's not the strongest or the most intelligent who will survive but those who can best manage change."

—Leon C. Megginson, professor at Louisiana State *University* (but often erroneously attributed to Charles Darwin)[72]

CHAPTER 4

. . . .

DEVELOPING DISRUPTIVE LEADERS

———————————●———————————

I N THE previous chapter, I showed that driving disruptive transformation requires leaders to start and sustain a movement that carries people through the tough times ahead. They must show up and establish credibility.

But what does it take to be a disruptive leader? Is being disruptive an innate quality, or can you systematically train yourself and others to become disruptive? This take on the age-old nature-versus-nurture question is crucial because if you want to create disruptive growth, you not only need to be a strong disruptive leader yourself, but also need disruptors sprinkled throughout your organization to make it happen. Out of necessity, you must hone your disruptor skills while also identifying potential other disruptors and nurturing them out of their comfort zones. There's no place for managers here. Everyone needs to be a leader.

To better understand what it takes for leaders to be disruptive, I conducted a global survey of more than a thousand leaders that revealed that not all disruptive leaders are alike. Although they share some common mindsets and behaviors, leaders manifest their disruptiveness in several ways—and need to be developed slightly differently too.

Before we delve more deeply into the characteristics and various kinds of disruptive leaders and how to develop them, let's take a look at an example of one from an unexpected place: the rarefied world of art museums.

GOING WHERE NO OTHER ART MUSEUM HAS GONE BEFORE

It was 2008, and Max Hollein, who was then the director of the venerable Städel Museum in Frankfurt, Germany, faced a critical challenge. Founded in 1816, the Städel was one of the oldest and most prestigious private art institutions in Germany. But attendance was in decline. Since he had previously transformed a sister museum in Frankfurt, the Schirn Kunsthalle, from a failing institution to hipster showcase, the board hoped that Hollein would work his magic and drive greater interest in the Städel too.

Hollein identified two parallel strategies to turn around the Städel. The first was to bring new exhibitions and acquire works for the museum, and then use digital channels to engage new audiences and bring depth to these exhibitions. The second was to build a $69 million wing for the Städel to make room for its growing contemporary art collection. Unfortunately, the timing was terrible: the museum broke ground on the new wing construction right after Lehman Brothers crashed in 2008. As one of the financial epicenters of Europe, Frankfurt was deeply affected by the financial crisis. At that point, Hollein had raised only half of the funds needed to finish the new wing.

Rather than take a cautious approach and stop construction and fundraising, Hollein pushed forward. "We created this momentum and at some point, people don't want this to fail because it would have been too embarrassing," he recalls.[73] "You might be forcing it against some people who are too cautious, but you have to always believe in it. You will never get 100 percent confirmation during such a process, and I guess I was never looking for that."

Hollein had the insight that Frankfurt is a city of citizens who have always been free to rule themselves. They love their museums and see them as a source of city pride. To be successful, Hollein knew he had to get the museum staff, Frankfurt citizens, and business leaders to buy into these changes and feel that they were a part of the success.

To generate interest and excitement, Hollein wore bright yellow construction boots everywhere and sold them to supporters for a donation as a symbol of building a museum together (see Figure 4.1).[74] The boots became a visible symbol of the change that was happening at the Städel, and they energized staff, donors, and volunteers to achieve audacious goals. In the end, half of the $69 million needed for the renovation came from private donors, with about $6 million from small individual donations.[75]

"The yellow boots were a symbol, not just of me wearing the boots but that the museum was built by all of us," Hollein explains. "The longer-lasting effect of the expansion campaign was to transform the relationship between the visitor and the institution into an extremely loyal and interested following that participates almost like a citizen of the museum."

> ## "Progress isn't achieved by preachers or guardians of morality, but by madmen, hermits, heretics, dreamers, rebels and sceptics"
> — Stephen Fry, English comedian, actor, and writer[76]

The results were astounding: the full $69 million fundraising goal was raised, with more than half of that coming from businesses or individuals. And attendance soared to a record-setting 447,395 visitors in 2012, up from its previous high of 328,773 visitors in 2009 before construction began—an increase of 36 percent.[77] Today the Städel relies on state funding for less than 15 percent of its budget, highly atypical for European museums.

From his posts in Frankfurt, Hollein moved on to become the director and CEO of the Fine Arts Museums of San Francisco, where he further developed an exhibit about the Teotihuacan pyramids,[78] complete with a Minecraft map that appealed to gamers and younger

Fig. 4.1 Städel Museum Director Max Hollein Fundraising in Yellow Boots

Source: Städel Museum

visitors, and an exhibit on contemporary Muslim fashion.[79] In 2018, he became the director of the Metropolitan Museum of Art, the largest art museum in the United States and the fourth most visited art museum in the world.[80] At the Met, he is working to ensure that the seventeen curatorial departments remain relevant in an increasing digital world while endeavoring to rebalance the Met's budget by 2020.

In many ways, Max Hollein was the perfect person to tackle a challenge like the Städel's. With degrees in both art history and business, he has a unique background to run art museums: he combines a sharp curatorial perspective with practical business execution and enviable fundraising skills. Although he pushes art patrons, employees, and museumgoers out of their comfort zone, he does so in a graceful way that both challenges and reassures them.

Hollein began developing the mindset and behaviors to be an effective leader of transformation in his first job out of school, serving as the chief of staff for the former Guggenheim Museum director, Thomas Krens. Hollein started working for him in 1995, taking on responsibility for fundraising and launching of the Guggenheim's expansion in Bilbao, Spain. "A portion of the board and certainly all of the journalists said that this was going to be a big failure, that it was a crazy idea," he shared.

But Hollein remembered watching Krens systematically address and disarm the critics. "You have to be not only a great communicator," Hollein told me as he reflected on what he picked up from Krens, "but you also have to create a narrative that's reassuring." He learned from Krens that he could push an ambitious agenda until the pieces fell into place and naysayers came around. Under Krens's wing, Hollein learned where and how to challenge the status quo while also developing a robust leadership tool kit for delivering results.

Hollein connects with people so that his cause not only becomes relevant to them but also energizes them to take action. He takes the time to listen closely to his staff. When Hollein joins a new museum, one of the first things he does is sit down with the curatorial lead of every department, asking them what exhibit they would like to put on if they had the time, people, and money.[81] While there's no promise to stage the exhibit, the simple act of asking and knowing these deep-rooted desires deepens the connection between Hollein and those he's leading.

In hindsight, Hollein's success as a museum director and transformation leader looks obvious, but it was not always an easy path. Hollein shared that there are typically two phases that he experiences when he begins a transformational change. "The first is the initial phase of the change, where you are looking at the possibilities, the options, the logic and you start to communicate, and you convince people," he explains. "And then there is the phase where you have to stay the course and be very quick in moving forward. I'm a strong believer in not getting distracted and using the momentum for a speedy implementation." Hollein's leadership style is to openly invite options, but then clearly define the way forward, eliminate deviations, and focus on execution.

As Hollein masters one set of challenges, he's driven to find more opportunities to improve and meet the mission of the museum because that is what energizes and sustains him. "Honestly, I love the feeling of being sometimes slightly overwhelmed because it allows me to focus and I can operate probably at my best," he admitted. "I become very calm and know that I have to make decisions. I thrive in those moments, so I probably need that kind of pressure."

Hollein is just one example of a highly effective transformational leader who pulls followers into an audacious journey of change. What are the mindsets and behavior he has in common with the other disruptive leaders so far detailed in this book?

THE MINDSET AND BEHAVIORS THAT MAKE A LEADER "DISRUPTIVE"

As the relationship between Hollein and his mentor, Thomas Krens, suggests, disruptive leaders learn from other disruptive leaders. But disruptive leaders must also teach those under them how to lead disruptive change too. No two disruptive leaders are exactly alike. Being disruptive is not binary; it's not something you either are or aren't. Rather, it's more of a continuum, ranging from having little desire to change the status quo to having a very strong drive to transform it. For that reason, understanding how disruptive leadership manifests differently is crucial not only to developing disruptive leaders but to identifying them in an organization.

The first step is understanding what it means to be disruptive leader. It's more than just a self-perception or an inclination to be disruptive. It's challenging the status quo and trying to change a situation for the better, which is crucial for leading disruptive growth. I'm not talking about change for the sake of change, but rather change to improve things. Being a disruptive leader is also not limited to formal leaders; informal leaders can be just as disruptive. I've long believed that leadership is a mindset, not a title.

I've had the good fortune to work with and observe many disruptive leaders over the past two decades and found that they share a few characteristics. At a high level, they exhibit the characteristics of "psychological hardiness," originally proposed by psychologists Salvatore Maddi and Suzanne Kobasa.[82] These leaders are high in "hardiness," that is, they are more likely to put stressful events into perspective. They perceive them as less of a threat and more as challenges and opportunities for personal development. Hardiness is made up of three attitudes:

Commitment refers to the belief in a higher purpose or truth, which results in disruptive leaders' ability to find meaning in their work and give it their best effort. Being committed to an outcome outside of themselves helps them see obstacles or bad news as minor setbacks. I consider being committed as the optimism that comes with thinking about a better future and that provides the perseverance to stick it out through tough times. Disruptive leaders use the vision of the future to develop commitment.

Control refers to leaders' beliefs that they can influence the events taking place around them with their efforts. In tough situations, they work to gain control over what they can by going into action rather than becoming overwhelmed by helplessness. At the same time, they recognize what they can't control and don't waste energy trying to control those things. Disruptive leaders possess not only confidence in themselves, but also in their followers' ability to execute when needed.

Challenge is the disposition to see problems as opportunities rather than as threats. Instead of becoming overwhelmed and defensive, disruptive leaders become curious and get busy looking for solutions. Because of their ability to deal with challenges, they believe that change, not predictability, is the norm. Disruptive leaders don't wait for the challenge to come to them; they seek it out.

"The most difficult thing is the decision to act, the rest is merely tenacity. The fears are paper tigers. You can do anything you decide to do. You can act to change and control your life; and the procedure, the process is its own reward."

—Amelia Earhart, aviator

As you can see, these three attitudes overlap and reinforce each other. Nevertheless, they don't solely explain the success of the disruptive leaders I've observed and studied. You could be psychologically hardy but never change the status quo.

To understand the drivers of disruptive leadership, I surveyed 1,087 leaders, primarily in the United States but also in Brazil, China, Germany, and the United Kingdom. I tested a slew of mindsets and leadership behaviors to understand which of them correlate with a higher disruption quotient —a measure of how much disruptive change leaders believe they are capable of leading.

Across all geographies, I found that the most effective disruptive leaders exhibited beliefs, traits, and behaviors that suggested a *mindset of openness to change*—that is, the ability to see change as an opportunity, not a setback— and a focus on *leadership behaviors that inspire and empower* followers—such as sharing a vision for the future while building a coalition of people to make the change happen. And these top beliefs, traits, and behaviors mapped really well with the three psychological hardiness characteristics (Figure 4.2):

For example, when it comes to commitment, disruptive leaders not only have a strong sense of purpose personally; they also craft and deploy manifestos (as I described in Chapter 3) to galvanize followers into committing to the cause. Their attitude regarding control is characterized by a tendency to be comfortable making a decision before having all the answers. And when it comes to challenges, disruptive leaders typically see failures as opportunities to learn from (which makes sense given that they actively seek out the unknown) and they encourage their people to find new ways to approach their work.[83]

Fig. 4.2 Top Drivers of Disruptive Leadership
by Hardiness Attitude

	OPENNESS TO CHANGE MINDSET	LEADERSHIP BEHAVIORS THAT INSPIRE AND EMPOWER FOLLOWERS
PSYCHOLOGICAL HARDINESS ATTITUDE — Commitment	• Constantly tries new things out of a belief that there's always something better	• Envisions exciting new possibilities for the organization • Interprets events to explain the urgent need for change
Control	• Comfortable with uncertainty and making a decision before having all the answers • Focuses on weighing which risks are worth taking	• Expresses confidence that people can attain challenging objectives • Encourages and facilitates innovation and entrepreneurship by others • Builds a coalition of key people to make change happen
Challenge	• Finds changes in routine interesting • Is energized by tackling new tasks at work or in personal life • Believes it's better to seek out the unknown • Believes mistakes and failure are an opportunity to learn • Believes change is the norm and creates opportunities for growth	• Looks beyond the boundaries of the organization to find ways to improve • Empowers people to try out new ways to approach their work • Encourages people to view problems or opportunities in a different way

THE FOUR ARCHETYPES OF DISRUPTIVE LEADERSHIP

Although there's no such thing as a good or bad disruptive leader, the pace and depth to which leaders are comfortable and capable of driving transformation vary significantly. My research centered on asking leaders how disruptive, defined as the ability to challenge the status quo and trying to change a situation for the better,[84] they were. What emerged from this analysis are four archetypes of disruptive leaders: the steadfast manager, the realist optimist, the worried skeptic, and the agent provocateur (see Figure 4.3).[85]

Fig. 4.3 **The Disruptive Leadership Archetypes**

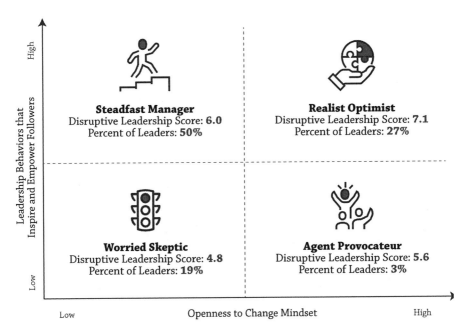

These four archetypes offer a deeper understanding and appreciation of the nuances of disruptive leadership. All leaders in your organization have some level of disruptive leadership in them, but some may not be as open to change or haven't developed the skill of leading through others. If you want to move your organization forward, you can go only as fast as your slowest leaders, so you want to have an honest conversation about where each of you stands.

The archetypes also provide a template for how leaders with different disruptive leadership capabilities can work with each other, as well as how to become more disruptive by more consistently adopting certain mindsets and behaviors. The archetypes answer not only the question of how to improve your disruption quotient or that of the leaders in your organization, but also why it's important to do so.

Finally, the archetypes can form the foundation for leadership development in your organization. They can be used not only to help leaders identify the mindsets and skills they need to work on, but also to identify high-potential disruptive leaders, regardless of their role or title. In my research, I found that disruptive leadership potential did not vary with age or role, meaning that it defies traditional leadership development programs that are designed specifically for a role.

Let's look at each of the archetypes and how they can work together to drive disruptive growth. (If you'd like to figure out your disruptive leadership archetype, visit charleneli.com/disruption-mindset for an online diagnostic.)

The Steadfast Manager

Steadfast Managers are the leaders the organization turns to when execution must happen on time and on budget—and they get it done with their team feeling empowered to figure out the right approach. They excel at clarifying roles and expectations while detailing the rules and procedures that will guide everyone's work. And people love working for them because these managers seek out their opinions and consult with them about decisions that may affect them.

They also spend much of their time and energy minimizing risk, reducing the chance that mistakes and failures plague the operations and success of their organization. Once they find something that works, they stick with it. While Steadfast Managers remain open to change, they believe it should be the exception. Their definition of success is that things run well, smoothly, and consistently.

When their organizations embark on a disruptive transformation strategy, Steadfast Managers often become uncomfortable with the shift in priorities. They feel the changes are unfair—as if all of the good work they had invested to deliver a smooth execution is no longer valued. In reality, they are the linchpin to any disruptive growth strategy. Without their strong leadership capabilities, especially in engaging their colleagues and establishing process and order, the work of disruptive growth won't get done.

Steadfast Managers do best partnering with Realist Optimists, who know how to put Steadfast Managers' strong leadership skills to work— and also understand how far they can stretch Steadfast Managers into disruptive change without stressing them out.

The Realist Optimist

Realist Optimists have what it takes to be highly effective disruptive leaders: a mindset that's open to change coupled with strong leadership behaviors that empower and inspire others to make change happen. They look at the world with a "glass is half-full" optimism; they believe there is a better solution and that it's only a matter of time until they find it!

Change and challenges don't stress them out. Just the opposite is the case: new situations energize them. When things go wrong, they take failure in stride, seeing it as an opportunity to learn and find a different way to meet their objective. Their capacity to grasp failure makes them realistic about the journey ahead, so they are prepared to rally their troops forward when the inevitable setbacks hit. Most important, they are confident in their ability to build a coalition of people to make change happen, fully realizing that they can't do it alone.

Their biggest challenge is that most leaders in their organization likely don't think the way they do. Realist Optimists stand out as the odd ducks. It's crucial that they find other Realist Optimists in the organization so they can amplify and support each other's agendas. They must also build a coalition with Steadfast Managers. But it's critical that Real Optimists help Steadfast Managers overcome their anxiety around change because their excellent leadership skills will be needed to rally the rest of the organization.

The Worried Skeptic

Worried Skeptics' nature is to look at the world from a glass-half-empty perspective and worry about all of the thing that can go wrong. And with good reason: they are often the leaders who get called when things blow up because they excel at cleaning up the mess. They are the hero of the moment, plugging the holes in the dam and calling for reinforcements.

They rely on their excellent analytical skills and intuition to work through problems rather than depend on inexperienced colleagues and team members to figure it out for themselves. Because the stakes are so high, they are skeptical of harebrained ideas that have not been thoroughly studied and backed up with data.

In an organization pursuing a disruptive strategy, it will sometimes feel that Worried Skeptics are the only sane people in the room—the only ones who can see the potential downside to a risky disruptive strategy. Their voice is crucial, and they should appeal to the strong leadership behaviors of the Realist Optimists to make sure that their concerns are heard and validated.

At the same time, Worried Skeptics need to improve their leadership behaviors to lead through others and become more curious about the disruptive growth initiatives being proposed— or they risk being left behind. They often find solace with Steadfast Managers who face similar challenges in being open to change. Having a kindred spirit who is going through the same disruptive leadership journey can be comforting.

The Agent Provocateur

With a big appetite for change and failure, Agents Provocateurs are on the front lines of disruption, constantly trying new things because they believe there's always something better than what they are doing today. They think it's better to seek out the unknown because change creates opportunities for growth. Routines bore them, so they take on new challenges at work and in their personal lives to become energized.

They often feel that others in their organization can't see or understand what the obvious opportunity is before them. And their biggest challenge is that while they want to advocate passionately for change, they find it challenging to get people involved and take action. To become more effective disruptive leaders, they must develop their ability to build a coalition of people who feel empowered to try new approaches to their work.

Agents Provocateurs must focus especially on establishing expectations and standards about the change they are pursuing, laying out detailed processes and procedures that provide guardrails for everyone to act in concert. In particular, they need to seek out Steadfast Managers in their organization. The leadership capabilities of Steadfast Managers, coupled with the openness to change and failure of Agents Provocateurs, make them a powerful combination to drive disruptive growth.

THE DISRUPTIVE LEADER GENDER GAP

I found that within each archetype, the average score for leadership behaviors and openness-to-change mindset were virtually the same across genders. That is, women feel just as capable as men in terms of their openness to change and in the leadership abilities to lead through others. But in the United States, male leaders' self-assessed disruption quotient scores—that is, how much disruptive change they *believe* they are capable of leading—were significantly higher than those of female leaders (see Figure 4.4).

Fig. 4.4 The Four Disruptive Leadership Archetypes, by Gender

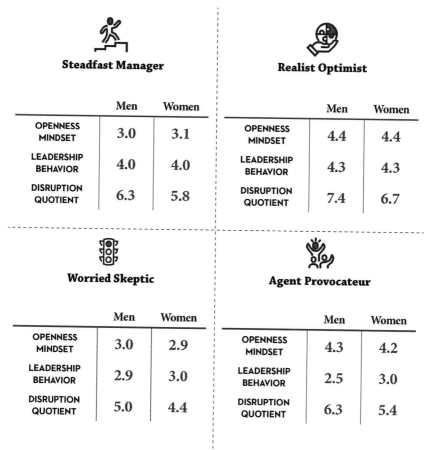

Steadfast Manager

	Men	Women
OPENNESS MINDSET	3.0	3.1
LEADERSHIP BEHAVIOR	4.0	4.0
DISRUPTION QUOTIENT	6.3	5.8

Realist Optimist

	Men	Women
OPENNESS MINDSET	4.4	4.4
LEADERSHIP BEHAVIOR	4.3	4.3
DISRUPTION QUOTIENT	7.4	6.7

Worried Skeptic

	Men	Women
OPENNESS MINDSET	3.0	2.9
LEADERSHIP BEHAVIOR	2.9	3.0
DISRUPTION QUOTIENT	5.0	4.4

Agent Provocateur

	Men	Women
OPENNESS MINDSET	4.3	4.2
LEADERSHIP BEHAVIOR	2.5	3.0
DISRUPTION QUOTIENT	6.3	5.4

Openness mindset scale from 1 (not comfortable with change at all) to 5 (highly comfortable with change). Leadership behavior—how often they engaged in a set of leadership behaviors—on a scale of 1 (never) to 5 (almost always).

This gender gap has significant implications for how we perceive, develop, and reward disruptive leaders. Because of societal and cultural expectations, we are not used to seeing women as "disruptive"; in fact, women don't see themselves as capable of challenging the status quo even though my research shows they are just as likely to have disruptive leadership mindsets and behaviors as men. In fact, being described--or even describing themselves--as disruptive may have negative connotations or, worse, consequences for them. As a woman, I have seen the unconscious bias that rewards us for being collaborative and congenial and the negative feedback that comes when we push for change against the status quo.

What's heartbreaking is that as a gender, we don't give ourselves as much permission to be disruptive leaders, even though at the core, we are as or more capable than our male counterparts.

DEVELOPING DISRUPTIVE LEADERSHIP IN YOURSELF AND OTHERS

Leaders step up to create positive change, so by definition, all leaders are disruptive to some extent. That means there is no "right" level of openness to change mindset or leadership behaviors that create change through others. I encourage you and your team to take the online diagnostic to learn what your disruptive leadership archetype is and to find out your scores for disruptive leadership mindsets and behaviors. Understanding what you and others score will help you identify where you need to improve or how to develop others so they can be great disruptive leaders too.

On one hand, leaders who have strong openness-to-change mindsets and leadership behaviors, but don't score high when it comes to seeing themselves as capable of leading disruption, may need coaching and mentoring to develop confidence in their ability to create disruptive transformation. My research shows that especially women might benefit from this kind of coaching and support.

On the other hand, some leaders see themselves as being very capable of leading disruption but show relatively average or lower openness-to-change mindsets and leadership behaviors that empower and inspire. If that's the case, the best practices that follow will help those leaders develop the mindset and behaviors they might lack. These practices are especially critical in our digital age when we frequently are not working face-to-face with the people we lead.

Commitment: Developing a Shared Vision and Purpose

Openness-to-Change Mindsets	Leadership Behaviors
◆ Constantly tries new things out of a belief that there's always something better	◆ Envisions exciting new possibilities for the organization ◆ Interprets events to explain the urgent need for change

Leaders are idealists and dreamers. They think about what is possible and encourage the people around them to be on the lookout for new opportunities. That's because the vision for a disruptive strategy doesn't come from sitting in a room staring at a crystal ball; it's sourced at the front lines from the people closest to your customers. Leaders find the common threads from these new possibilities and translate them into a purpose, a "why" that others can commit to. Here are a few ways to sharpen the mindsets and behaviors that will help you and the leaders you are developing craft a shared vision and purpose for your disruptive transformation:

Encourage dreaming. Do you give yourself and others permission to dream? Or do you think it's a frivolous act? You won't try new things if you don't believe that things can be better, so dreaming is the first step to identifying possibilities. Leaders like John Legere at T-Mobile use digital and social platforms to inspire both customers and employees to dream of a better future.

Mirror back their deepest desires. The vision you create becomes shared only if it reflects back to your colleagues and customers what they most desire. And for most of us, what we desire the most is meaning, not money. We want to know that in the time we spend on this earth, we have made a difference. The best disruptive leaders tap into this longing by explaining the purpose so that people understand their role in achieving it. Max Hollein sought out and listened to curatorial department leaders to understand their deepest hopes and desires and inspire them to think bigger and deeper.

Look farther down the road to go faster. In this fast-changing digital world, it may seem insane to be crafting a vision five or more years out when you can't predict even what will happen this month! But when you drive at high speeds on the highway, you have to look out far ahead of your car to see the curves and obstacles and make the adjustments now. That future vision gives you the context and urgency to take action today.

Control: Creating Stability and Ownership

Openness-to-Change Mindsets	Leadership Behaviors
• Comfortable with uncertainty and making a decision before having all the answers • Focuses on weighing which risks are worth taking	• Expresses confidence that people can attain challenging objectives • Encourages and facilitates innovation and entrepreneurship by others • Builds a coalition of key people to make change happen

One of the biggest problems created by disruptive transformation is the tremendous uncertainty that makes you feel as if you are not in control of the situation. There are so many unknowns, things are changing quickly, and simply staying on top of what is happening is all you can do. This is where control becomes important on two fronts.

First is how you exert control over your own emotions and shift your mindset when things are spinning out of control around you. Leaders with strong control can dampen down their instinctual reaction to chaos and uncertainty, and through the act of making decisions, they begin to have control. They are not frozen into indecision by uncertainty. Instead they understand that swift decision making will reduce the uncertainty. Even if the decision ends up in a failure, they are better off knowing that it doesn't work than staying back where they were before.

Second is how you give that sense of control to your followers. By defining where your followers are empowered to take actions—where they have ownership and permission to act—they gain control. This sense of control is essential, because if you and your team believe that you can control the outcomes of your disruptive transformation, then you'll throw everything at it to make it happen. But if your team believes it has no control or influence over the outcomes, they will stand helpless on the sidelines, hoping that the storm will blow by and miss them.

To increase your and your organization's ability to step into power and control a situation, consider these best practices:

Iterate and prepare for worst-case scenarios. The beauty of worst-case scenarios is that they give a name to the unspeakable. By anticipating and preparing for what could go wrong, you're visualizing you and your team in these stressful situations. This allows you to understand and interpret the data and situations and focus on weighing which risks are worth taking. When the tough times come, you already know what you can and can't do to influence the outcome, and you've given yourself the time and presence of mind to see the opportunities that the change offers.

Conduct better postmortems. Nothing ever goes perfectly, so use postmortems after a project or quarter ends to identify what you could have done differently. One best practice is to spend a quarter of your time in the postmortem on examining what went wrong, a quarter of the time discussing what you learned, and the rest of time talking about what you will do next. Make sure everyone on the team contributes, use digital tools that support anonymous commenting and questioning to facilitate honest observations, distribute the notes to everyone, and start your next project or quarter with a review of the agreed steps. Having a plan will increase your sense of control in fast-moving times.

Give permission—and forgiveness—freely. "Don't ask for permission, beg for forgiveness" sounds great, but in reality, we've been trained since kindergarten to raise our hands to ask for permission. The top reason leaders give for not leading disruptive change is that they don't believe they have permission to do so. This is at all levels of the organization, even in the C-suite (they typically blame the CEO or the board). As a leader, give permission constantly and frequently, and make a big show of forgiving as well as encouraging the entrepreneurial heart that beats in everyone. If you are waiting for permission yourself, stop. Check if permission really is needed. Even if it is, figure out if your relationship is strong enough for you to ask for forgiveness later instead.

Create support networks. Change is hard work and disruptive transformation is exhausting and lonely. Find the key people in your organization who will help you carry the torch of change because you will need a break to recover. Supplement with people outside your organization through online communities or attend conferences to learn from the programming and build your network of fellow disruptors.[86]

Challenge: Recasting Failure

Openness-to-Change Mindsets	Leadership Behaviors
◆ Finds changes in routine interesting ◆ Is energized by tackling new tasks at work or in personal life ◆ Believes it's better to seek out the unknown ◆ Believes mistakes and failure are an opportunity to learn ◆ Believes change is the norm and creates opportunities for growth	◆ Looks beyond the boundaries of the organization to find ways to improve ◆ Empowers people to try out new ways to approach their work ◆ Encourages people to view problems or opportunities in a different way

One of my favorite sayings is, "Experience is what you get when you don't get what you want." It's only when you make mistakes and fail that you learn. And yet I can't tell you how many times I've met highly accomplished leaders who secretly admit to me that they are terrified of failing. They spend a huge amount of energy trying to avoid failure or at least the appearance of it. I am not advocating that you intentionally fail, but rather that you recast failure as an opportunity to learn.

Several colleges now include classes on how to learn from failure in their curricula.[87] And the "agile" process that many tech companies embrace consists of many iterative test-and-learn (*not* test-and-fail) cycles. (For more information about what I call "The Failure Imperative," check out Chapter 9 in my book, *Open Leadership*.[88]) To develop for either yourself or others the mindsets and behavior associated with recasting failure, follow these best practices:

Plan little experiments to foster curiosity. As a leader, you are a natural experimenter; you try new approaches to solve problems all the time. When you identify an area where you or your organization is being resistant to change, plan an experiment where the outcome is uncertain but the perceived risk is low. The goal here is to create a sense of curiosity about the unknown and the freedom to experiment to figure it out. With each iteration, push for bigger experiments to increase your ability to deal with bigger, hairier uncertainties.

Search for flow. Some of you may have experienced "flow"—that moment when you are so absorbed and focused on your task that you slip into effortless and optimal performance. Flow is possible only when your skills are stretched to meet a challenge. Too much challenge and you are stressed and anxious; too little challenge and you fall into boredom and apathy. Disruptive leaders look for challenges that stretch and test their and their team's skills because that's when they feel accomplished and excellent.

Practice optimism. Are you problem focused or solution oriented? In a survival situation, people who most often perish say, "Oh, no! We're all going to die!" But people who survive ask, "What is the next step I need to take to get out of this situation?" For those of you who are not wired to see the glass as half-full, partner with a compatible optimist so that you share your different perspectives of the same situation. Exposure to a different mindset is the first step to changing your own perceptions.

Create a "failure résumé." We all have stunning professional résumés that tout our many successes. But cataloging what we've learned from our failures is just as valuable.[89] Think back to your most stunning failures. What did you learn? How are you better off today because of that failure? Write your answers down. And as you continue to fail, keep capturing your failures, along with observations and analysis on what lead to them. By stepping back and taking stock, you learn and build on each failure as you move toward success.

MOVING FORWARD

Now that you know what it takes to be a disruptive leader, I urge you to develop more of these leaders. My research found that while many leaders exhibit an openness-to-change mindset and the leadership behaviors to empower and inspire others, there is a significant gap in the confidence these leaders have in their disruption ability, especially in the case of women.

This should be a cause for concern: we have fewer leaders psychologically ready to step forward to drive disruptive transformation at a time when we most need them to do so. Don't count on millennials to take the charge either. I have found that they are no more likely than other generations to see themselves as disruptive. And if you are in a large organization, the urgency is most dire: the lowest disruptive quotient scores came from organizations that are large. So don't wait. Identify disruptive leaders, and help them develop the mindsets and behaviors they will need to drive breakthrough growth in your organization.

TAKEAWAYS

- Being a disruptive leader means having confidence in your ability to challenge the status quo and change a situation for the better. The biggest drivers of disruptive leadership are an openness-to-change mindset and leadership behaviors that empower and inspire followers.
- The four archetypes of disruptive leaders can help you assess and understand what kind of disruptive leader you and your counterparts in the organization are and how to work together.
- Take special note that women perceive themselves as being significantly less disruptive than their male counterparts, despite having the same or better levels of openness-to-change mindset and leadership behaviors that empower and inspire followers.

"Culture eats strategy for breakfast every day."

—Attributed to Peter Drucker

CHAPTER 5
. . . .
DISRUPTING YOUR CULTURE

———————————●———————————

BEING ON the right side of disruption requires having not just the right strategy but also the culture and leadership to execute it. Culture determines how much disruptive transformation your organization can create. It is either the limiting factor or the growth engine. All-too-many organizations shy away from breakthrough strategies because they don't believe they can change their organizational culture. You don't want to be one of them.

As your strategy shifts to address new growth opportunities, the way that you work will most likely have to change as well, and your culture will have to as well. So the right question to ask is *how*—not *if*—you have to change your culture to create, drive, and sustain your disruptive transformation strategy.

The ultimate goal isn't to transform your culture to some ideal, "perfect" one that drives breakthrough growth. There is no such thing. The goal is to develop a culture that thrives on the three beliefs necessary to chase after your fastest-moving customers: openness, agency, and agility.

And here's the gritty truth: you will have to constantly disrupt and transform your culture as your strategy changes. Disruption is not for the faint of heart and requires discipline, process, and united leadership.

But the reward is an organization that thrives on meeting challenges rather than one that cowers in the face of change, as McKinsey and Company found out in 2010.

HOW MCKINSEY TRANSFORMED ITSELF

McKinsey and Company is arguably one of the most prestigious management consulting companies in the world. It has a culture that reaches back to the 1950s when the firm's managing director, Marvin Bower, established a set of principles that govern decisions and behavior, from working only with CEOs to always acting in the best interest of clients ahead of the Firm.[90]

When Dominic Barton took over as the global managing director of McKinsey in 2009, the firm faced a world that was rapidly changing—but McKinsey wasn't. The last strategy review had taken place twelve years earlier. Barton remembered that one of the major initiatives of the review was to change the way projects were delivered. At the time, client needs were almost always served with a model of an engagement manager (EM) and two associates. This "EM+2" model was almost exactly the same as it was twelve years prior. "Everyone was well intended but not much had changed," Barton remarked. [91]

Barton set out to do a new strategy review, and from the start, he made it clear what was up for evaluation and what was out of bounds. "We didn't want to change our mission statement and values, things like putting clients first and attracting exceptional people," he told me. "But everything else in terms of who we serve, how we serve them, how we're paid, who we recruit—we should just list these orthodoxies out and challenge them by asking, 'Why? Does that make sense today given the changes that are going on?'"

Barton's strategy process systematically challenged orthodoxies at McKinsey. For example, the strategy team, led by ten senior partners, asked why McKinsey served only the 500 biggest companies in the world. How about working with fast-growing tech companies when they were still small? Or what if the firm got into helping implement the strategies on behalf of clients? That would require hiring people with more extensive experience running plants, hospital chains, or retail stores. And that led to a bigger question of why McKinsey previously hired only MBAs from a small set of schools from around the world rather than experienced professionals in specific fields.

By late 2010, Barton's strategy effort had identified ten major initiatives that represented radical departures from the firm's established practices. To implement them, he needed approval from the firm's 350 senior partners, who were gathered in a hotel conference room in Boston. The scene was chaotic, Barton recalled. "People would come out of the breakout groups going, 'Dom, this is a really, really good idea. If we don't do it, I'm not sure I want to stay in the firm." And from the same room, other people were saying, 'This idea is so bad. If we do it, I'm not sure if I want to be in this firm.'"

That was when the former global managing director, Fred Gluck, stood on a chair, banged a glass with a spoon to get everyone's attention, and said, "I want to remind everyone that partnership is not about consensus. It is about trust. Even if we're not in agreement, we trust each other to act in the best interest of the firm."

The vote on several of the initiatives was close, barely passing with a majority, but they passed. Barton implemented those initiatives and then continued to find ways to challenge orthodoxies, regularly jolting the organization to get out of its complacency and to look at serving clients in new ways. One of the last jolts he implemented just before he left the managing partner role was to hire five people into consulting roles at McKinsey who did not have college degrees.

Barton admitted that it was far from easy to transform the venerable firm. "We love to tell other people to change, but it's not fun when you're the one changing." But he also shared that the people at McKinsey started behaving differently. "A lot of people just felt released. They'd say, 'I've wanted to do something like this,' or 'I can now do more with my clients.' We were giving people more tools and openings to try different things to help their clients. More people could be successful, and then we began to see it in the growth."

McKinsey increased its annual growth rate from a modest 2 to 3 percent a year to about 12 to 15 percent during this period. This growth was not easy, though. Recent media focus on work done in South Africa, Saudi Arabia, and China has brought scrutiny to the firm.[92] But I'm a believer that McKinsey is better able to tackle these challenges because it's already strong from having internally challenged itself.

Just like McKinsey, disruptive organizations have to systematically and intentionally disrupt their culture to transform their organizations and drive disruptive growth. But what exactly is culture, and how does it become the engine that can fast-track your disruptive transformation?

THE BELIEFS OF FLUX CULTURES

Culture is the shared understanding of "how we do things around here." Everyone in your company knows and feels your culture every day. They know if risk taking is truly valued and encouraged—or if it's just words on the wall. They know whether it's safe to challenge authority or if it's a career-ending move. And they know if they can get away with not following a specific process or if they will feel accountable to meet high standards. While you can point to specific structures, processes, and policies that define how work gets done, there are also many elements of how we work that don't live on paper. Culture, for example, lives in the minds and hearts of each employee. It is emotionally felt rather than logically and rationally managed.

There are no "good" or "bad" cultures. One organization can be extremely competitive, with dueling teams battling out to get their approach adopted. Another makes decisions on a consensus basis. What works in one company is anathema in another.

Simply put, culture is a set of beliefs and behaviors that define how work gets done, of what is appropriate and what is not (see Figure 5.1). Beliefs are the shared assumptions that people bring to work every day and that manifest throughout the organization as "things that we hold to be true." Behaviors are the things that people do every day to get work done: the words that we say and the actions we take. They come from our beliefs about how work ought to get done and in turn reinforce such beliefs. Cultural elements—organizational structures, processes, policies, rituals, symbols, and stories—are *manifestations* and *expressions* of a culture's underlying beliefs. That's why just putting in place new cultural elements, like a new department structure, or mandating new behaviors, like taking more risks, make little impact unless they reflect a fundamental change in the underlying beliefs.

Fig. 5.1 Beliefs and Behaviors Define an Organization's Culture

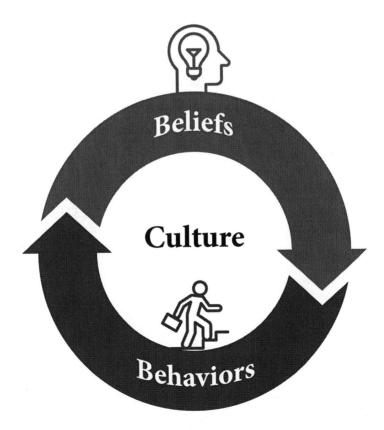

Beliefs and behaviors evolve over time, and not always for the better. One organization I worked with had a company value of respect, grounded in the belief that people need to show respect to each other. Over time, "respect" morphed with the belief that everyone had to offer their ideas and agree before a decision could move forward. Eventually people started keeping their opinions to themselves since challenging others was interpreted as a sign of disrespect.

Faced with increasing competitive pressure and faster product cycles, the company's leaders realized they couldn't continue operating in this way. So they redefined what the value "respect" meant for them. They demonstrated how to engage in respectful disagreement, strengthening their commitment to each other and the company regardless of whether the outcome was the one that they advocated. They developed a new belief that leadership had respect for people's expertise and judgment and their ability to make decisions without having to seek approval for everything. And most important, the organization trained leaders to seek out, encourage, and recognize diverse and dissident opinions throughout the organization. By systematically identifying and changing this one cultural element—the value of respect—that was holding them back, the organization was able to work better and faster toward achieving its audacious transformation goals.

As this organization found out, if a disruptive transformation strategy is the road your organization must navigate, then culture is the engine that determines how fast you'll travel along the road. Every element of your culture will either pin you to the status quo or propel you forward to a disruptive growth future.

I've given cultures that seem to live in a state of perpetual flux and thrive a nickname: flux cultures. Disruptive transformation demands new beliefs and behaviors that fly in the face of those typically promoted in most corporate cultures, which traditionally focus on operational excellence and efficiency. Flux cultures instead build a foundation of trust and safety, giving people the emotional strength to confidently push into the unknown and take audacious risks. People will disrupt and radically transform how they work and do things only if they feel safe, because emotions, not logic, drive change. They must believe that if they stretch and take a risk, their colleagues and company will be there to catch and support them. A flux culture provides that safety net. The opposite is a "stuck culture," one that is stuck in the status quo and fails to nurture its employees' ability to handle the kind of massive change that's needed to support a disruptive strategy. The beliefs of stuck and flux cultures are polar opposites (see Figure 5.2).

Fig. 5.2 How Stuck and Flux Cultures Approach Challenge Differently

Stuck Culture Beliefs	Flux Culture Beliefs
"This is the way we've always done it."	"There's got to be a better way."
Knowledge is power, so hoard information to make everyone come to you.	Sharing is power; spread information to empower people to act.
Information is shared only on a need-to-know basis.	Information is shared except on a need-to-keep secret basis.
People are confident that what works today will in the future.	People are paranoid that what works today won't in the future.
Tests are used to be proven right.	Tests are used to be proven wrong—so you know where to improve.
Everyone follows the chain of command.	People are comfortable talking to their boss's boss as needed.
If it's not invented here, then it can't be good.	People are curious about new possibilities.
People tend to be thin-skinned and can't stand being challenged.	People tend to be thick-skinned; they enjoy being challenged.

In my research, I found as many different types of disruptive flux cultures as there are disruptive transformation strategies and saw that there isn't a perfect culture to drive breakthrough growth. But I have found three beliefs that appear in flux cultures and organizations, regardless of their size or industry: openness, agency, and action (see Figure 5.3). These three beliefs are the secret sauce that enable disruptive organizations to live in a perpetual state of flux and see challenges as opportunities rather than as obstacles.

Fig. 5.3 **The Three Beliefs of Flux Cultures**

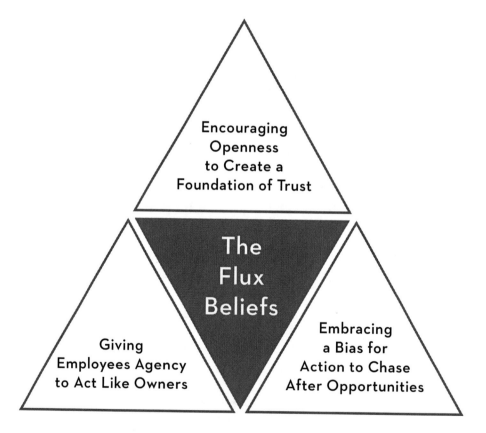

Let's take a closer look at each of the flux beliefs, starting with using openness to create a foundation of trust.

THE OPENNESS BELIEF: CREATE A FOUNDATION OF TRUST

In my previous book, *Open Leadership*, I defined two types of openness that exist within organizations.[93] The first is the availability of information—how freely the organization shares things like financial reports on how the organization is doing or detailed data about how customers are engaging. The more information that is available and the faster it flows, the more likely it is that the organization can make use of it to drive disruptive transformation. For example, understanding customers is typically the job of market research. But if customer interactions from sales and service can be collected and analyzed, the information can be used to understand subtle shifts in the landscape that may warrant an early response.

In organizations that are open, information doesn't just flow faster from the bottom up; it also flows more frequently from the top down. There is a shift from a mindset of "need to know," where large amounts of information have restricted access, to one of "need to keep private," where only a small subset of data such as salary information or legal proceedings is guarded.[94] These organizations also share more openly not just their successes but also their problems and setbacks. They believe that the more people know about them, the better able they are to overcome obstacles.

The second way that openness manifests in organizations is in the decision-making process. Clarifying how decisions are made—the data and criteria used, who participates, the options weighed—increases the likelihood that people affected by a decision will support it. One organization I worked with decided to make most of its meetings open to anyone who wanted to attend if they felt it would be helpful to their work. This meant that each meeting had to have clear agendas and outcomes. More transparency gave everyone the confidence that each leader was moving and changing in coordination with everyone else.

In organizations that are open, decisions from the top down are more visible, and the decision-making process is also more participatory. Digital collaboration platforms have made it possible for ideas to come from any corner of the organization and be visible to everyone. Once surfaced, these ideas are no longer constrained by hierarchical paths: whoever wants to take one or more up can do so and bring them to life. For example, one person at a company posted the idea of replacing paper coffee cups with mugs, and the following week, the marketing department delivered boxes of unused promotion mugs around the office. This may seem like a small example, but it shows the power of making information and decision making open to everyone.

When you are pursuing disruptive transformation, openness is especially important for the following reasons:

It creates accountability. Legendary investor Warren Buffett has a saying, "Only when the tide goes out do you discover who's been swimming naked." When there is no place to hide, your success and failures become readily available to everyone in the organization. There is no place for backroom lobbying or politics, where personal relationships trump facts and data. High performers get the recognition they deserve, mediocre performers up their game, and poor performers get ousted. Transparency clears the air and creates a single version of the truth that everyone sees and agrees is real.

It forces difficult conversations. A commitment to openness forces uncomfortable conversations to happen, addressing the elephant in the room that everyone knows about but doesn't want to deal with. Clearing the air of hidden agendas and unsaid feedback creates confidence that there is nothing left that stands between us. Hedge fund Bridgewater practices a form of "radical transparency," encouraging people to tell each other the things that are hardest to share. Its CEO, Ray Dalio, wrote in his book, *Principles*, "Create an environment in which everyone has the right to understand what makes sense and no one has the right to hold a critical opinion without speaking up."[95] This can happen only if there is trust that being honest about your opinion won't come back to bite you.

It removes fear of failure. Learning happens when mistakes are made, attempts fail, and pilot tests crash. Unless these failures are shared openly and widely, each person is limited to learning only from his or her own experiences. Rather than spending precious energy defensively covering up problems and setbacks, openness encourages people to come forward by acknowledging the value of the learning that came from the failure.

It creates opportunities for diversity perspectives to filter up. The more open an organization is, the more likely it will see more possibilities in everything around it. Things literally begin to look different because people from different departments, levels, geographic areas, or backgrounds all process information differently and bring different perspectives to decision making as well.

While being open has these benefits, it is hard! As businesspeople, we've been trained over our careers to believe just the opposite: that keeping things secret is safer, that sharing is dangerous, that information gives you power. We fear that being more open means giving up control. But just the opposite happens: you gain power when you decide how to delegate information access and decision-making rights. By shifting responsibility and accountability to others, you earn credibility and gain their trust—and that puts you in a better position to create bigger change with greater impact and have influence at a larger scale.

Continuous openness creates a sense of trust that there are no hidden agendas and that you trust your colleagues to be honest with you about any concerns or setbacks. The more audacious and disruptive your transformation is, the more openness and trust you need to build into relationships that will hold your organization together through the change.

How open should you be? How open do you need to be to support your disruptive growth strategy? My answer is to ask a different question: How much do you need to trust your team to use information and make decisions in pursuit of your disruption strategy? You will move faster as you build more trust with openness. The only brake being put on this is your own personal comfort level with how open you are. Whatever that comfort zone is, stretch a little beyond that, and don't let concerns about control cloud your ability to use sharing to develop trust.

Case Study: Nokia

By the time Risto Siilasmaa took over as Nokia chairman in mid-2012, the company had already lost 90 percent of its stock value due to a misplayed consumer handset strategy. Making the handset business work would require a cash infusion that Nokia did not have, so Siilasmaa and Nokia's CEO at the time, Stephen Elop, worked closely to uncover emerging growth opportunities in the broader information and communications technology (ICT) space. They decided that the best choice was to sell the handset business and transform the company into a new business focused on telecom equipment and service rather than consumer electronics.

Making this transformation was fraught with many obstacles, the biggest being that Nokia was emotionally and financially the pride of Finland. It seemed unthinkable for the company to exit the handset business. As a successful entrepreneur, Siilasmaa knew that one of the ways to move successfully through huge changes was to be more open. In his book, *Transforming Nokia,* he wrote, "When the worst possible outcome could be talked about, it actually removes the fear and then we can plan and prepare ourselves."[96]

Being open was a sharp departure from where Nokia was operating. When Siilasmaa joined the Nokia board in 2008, he was a successful Finnish tech entrepreneur and was dazzled by the prospect of joining the storied company's board. But at his first board meeting, he was surprised that there wasn't even a mention about the new iPhone or Android, which had just been launched in the past year.

He soon realized that the management team wasn't sharing the full picture of Nokia's declining competitiveness and that the board wasn't holding them accountable. "If we had had visibility," he told me, "we would've seen that competitiveness was declining rapidly and we would have seen some of the root causes of that decline. Data would have given us the tools to understand what was really happening inside the company."

When Siilasmaa became board chair, he was determined to make changes. "We were tired of being surprised by negative news on topics that we should not have been surprised by," he explained. He instituted a new mantra: "No news is bad news. Bad news is good news. Good news is no news." He explained further, "When we don't feel that we have to hide the possible negative futures, the risks, failures, and mistakes, then we trust each other more."

Siilasmaa also used transparency to keep people involved, asking them for their ideas and sharing almost in real time what happened in discussions where they were not involved. He insisted that updates from morning meetings be shared by noon and afternoon meeting outcomes shared by the end of the day. By being open and transparent, he was slowly building a new culture of trust.

Trust was going to be needed in heaping servings because Nokia was pursuing two complex transactions at the same time. Microsoft CEO Steve Ballmer approached Siilasmaa to discuss selling the handset business to the tech giant.[97] Meanwhile, Nokia was talking with Siemens about buying the Siemens part of Nokia Siemens that it didn't already own. To manage the complexity, Siilasmaa implemented a rigorous scenario planning process to identify their strategic options. The discipline of this planning forced a new behavior: up and down throughout the organization, teams and people were developing multiple options and outcome scenarios, sharing information and making decisions at all levels.

While many acquisition talks are like mini-soap operas, these two transactions were extraordinary given they were happening simultaneously. The Microsoft transaction itself saw three rounds of negotiations break down over the course of a year. At one point, the Microsoft board rejected the deal Nokia had negotiated with Ballmer. "When Steve [Ballmer] called me and told me that their board had turned the deal down, I thought, 'Okay, it didn't happen the way we wanted; we'll figure out another way to get this done,'" Siilasmaa told me. The preparation, the scenarios, and the trust he had built with the board and management team gave him the confidence that they could pivot, shift, and transform based on whatever was thrown at them. Throughout this period, Siilasmaa kept communicating and sharing information consistently. The board and board committees, in fact, met over one hundred times in less than two years; in 2013 alone, they had sixty-four board and board committee meetings.

In the end, Nokia sold the handset business to Microsoft, bought Siemen's half of Nokia Siemen, and acquired the French telecommunications equipment company Alcatel Lucent. Today Nokia is the second largest telecommunications infrastructure company in the world, with €22.6 billion in revenues in 2018 and 102,000 employees. Of those employees, only 5 percent carried a Nokia badge in 2013. Nokia's transformation represents one of the most audacious and astounding transformation I've seen in modern business.

Developing an Open Culture

While not all transformations will be as dramatic as Nokia's, openness can build a foundation of trust for your organization. Here are some best practices:

Create a safe and inclusive environment. Regular communications and meetings like all-hands meetings, email updates, weekly conference calls, and so on are great, but unless they show a commitment to including people's ideas in a safe space, they won't be effective. For example, if you have regular meetings, allow people to submit questions anonymously in advance and in real-time and commit to answering every question, time permitting. Or provide a way for people to give continuous anonymous feedback and publicly address their submitted questions or concerns. As you address these anonymous but sometimes tough questions, you are demonstrating that people can trust that there will be little retribution for raising difficult topics, which will encourage more openness of information sharing and building trust.

Identify crucial places where trust is low, and address it with openness. If malaise hangs over a stuck organization, go right to the core of the problem: Where would trust make the biggest impact? Work with the affected teams to deepen a belief in openness and develop better ways of sharing. Trust will come, slowly at first, as you insist and persist on being open.

Put vital data and information where they can be best used. Make sure that the data that will most sway a decision are readily available to the people who need it. One organization realized that it had key customer data buried in an enterprise platform that was accessible only to the market research team. Giving read-only access to anyone working on customer-facing initiatives sent the signal that employees throughout the company were entrusted with using customer analytics wisely. This isn't about creating a 360-degree view of the customer, but strategically identifying information that your organization already has and putting it in the hands of people who can use it to create impact.

Jump-start enterprise collaboration platforms to encourage sharing. Among the most underused and underappreciated tools in an organization are enterprise collaboration tools and platforms, like SharePoint, Teams, and Slack. I once worked with a hot "unicorn" start-up in Silicon Valley whose collaboration platform was stagnant: not a single executive had used the platform in over a month. Sharing needs to start at the top, so encourage your executives to find ways to share updates on how things are going, provide insight into how decisions are made, and solicit questions to create engagement. All of these actions will break down the power distance that naturally exists between levels and build stronger trust within the organization.

Measure openness and trust in your culture. As an engineer, Nokia's Siilasmaa loves to measure things and rose to the challenge of measuring Nokia's change in culture. For example, he measures how hierarchical the organization is by asking people how comfortable they are talking to their boss's boss. "It's not supposed to be easy to do this," he explains, "but if there's trust, then it should be a pragmatic matter to just talk to the person who is above your direct boss." You don't need to measure everything—just a few behaviors that indicate that your efforts to create a more open, trust-based culture are working.

Use collaboration platforms to facilitate the flow of information. One of the biggest changes in the workplace is the emergence of online collaboration platforms that allow people to exchange information and ideas with less friction. In *The Engaged Leader*, I shared the story of how David Thodey, the CEO of Australian telecommunication leader Telstra, asked employees to share the top time-wasting and unnecessary approval processes that were slowing the organization and committed to either fixing them or explaining why they existed. Within the first hour, 700 submissions came in! It may be easier for people, especially those earlier in their career and not in a position of power, to feel safe or comfortable sharing information online or anonymously.

THE AGENCY BELIEF: GIVING PERMISSION TO ACT LIKE OWNERS

Recently a team I worked with proudly shared that they were moving faster now that their leader had committed to attend their work group meetings. By being present, he could make decisions on their recommendations in real time. My first question was whether the leader had ever disagreed with any of their recommendations. "No, he approved every one of them." My second question was whether the leader's participation in these meetings had influenced their recommendations. "No. We had already gotten feedback through other channels; we just needed his approval." My third question was really an observation: Why did they even bother going through this approval process in the first place?

This team had fallen prisoner to a common belief that all decisions had to be approved by higher-ups.

In my workshops with organizations, I hear over and over again from managers and employees that they don't have permission to take independent action or make changes they think are necessary without approval from someone else. What a shame. When you are trying to catch up to your fast-moving customers you need everyone to move as quickly as possible. You can't afford to have them held back by unnecessary gatekeepers.

Organizations that believe in giving all their employees agency, that is, the capacity to act independently and make their own choices, help them see themselves as owners and leaders of their transformation strategy. When they identify a need for change, they make it happen—and do so regardless of their actual title or role. People who have been given agency feel a responsibility to think about the good of the overall organization and make decisions based on its long-term interests.

Agency is more than empowerment, which is the power that comes from leaders at the top to employees at the bottom. Agency is a two-way street: power comes with responsibility and accountability.

Organizations that give their employees a strong sense of agency over decisions make this understanding explicit: if you get to make a decision, you will also be accountable for it. As a result, these employees exhibit the following behaviors:

- They never use the excuse "that wasn't my job" to explain why something failed. Instead, they seek out the people and resources to get something done, often breaking through department or cultural walls.

- They consider the impact of their decisions on customers and other teams over time. They are willing to do with less for themselves and the immediate team if it means a larger benefit to the organization over the long term.

- They think about future needs and outcomes, such as building a foundation for future scale, identifying and investing in emerging customers, and finding and developing great talent.

Agency also smooths the power dynamics of hierarchies. I've seen transformation strategies grind to a halt because the teams executing them needed to get buy-in from top executives in order to move forward. This is the malaise of many organizations, which defaults to what I call HIPPO ("highest-paid-person's opinion"). Rather than basing a decision on customer data and honest debate, they go with whatever the boss decides.

But when agency exists throughout the organization, the "boss" isn't the manager or the executive up the chain; customers ultimately are. While you can and should challenge your team members' recommendations, you must base your challenge on an understanding of customer needs—and not just on your gut. Your employees shouldn't have to compromise in order to appease an executive somewhere in the chain of command.

Of course, when you give people in your organization agency, you also need to be prepared to fully support their ideas, even if you disagree with them. Think about all the energy wasted on internal politics being channeled instead to deciding on the best outcome for your customers.

Any disruptive transformation effort worth doing is going to be controversial, risky, and not a slam dunk. And once a decision is made to go in a direction, everyone must be able to set aside their differences and support the decision, even if they disagree with it. It's especially crucial that you get 100 percent behind the new direction. Unfettered support shows you respect that they are owners of the decision. They need to know that you will have their back and will support them through thick and thin. They need to trust that you will work hard to make the initiative a success, not sit on the sidelines, waiting for it to fail and the opportunity to say, "I told you so."

Let's take a closer look at how one organization instills agency in its people.

Case Study: Amazon

Amazon has fourteen "Leadership Principles" that serve as the foundation for the company's strategy and culture.[98] They appear prominently on the Amazon Careers website. Two of those leadership principles get at the heart of what it means to give your people a sense of agency over decisions.

The first principle is "Ownership," which Amazon defines in this way: "Leaders are owners. They think long term and don't sacrifice long-term value for short-term results. They act on behalf of the entire company, beyond just their own team. They never say, 'that's not my job.'" That principle is manifested in how employees talk about their work: they don't describe what they do; rather, they describe what they *own*. They own a technology, an experience, a process. They are responsible when what they own works, and when it doesn't.

The second principle is "Have Backbone; Disagree and Commit." This is how Amazon defines that principle: "Leaders are obligated to respectfully challenge decisions when they disagree, even when doing so is uncomfortable or exhausting. Leaders have conviction and are tenacious. They do not compromise for the sake of social cohesion. Once a decision is determined, they commit wholly."

In his 2016 letter to shareholders, Amazon CEO Jeff Bezos expanded on what the "Disagree and Commit" principle is. [99] I'm including the full text from that letter because no one explains this concept better than Bezos himself:

> *If you have conviction on a particular direction even though there's no consensus, it's helpful to say, "Look, I know we disagree on this, but will you gamble with me on it? Disagree and commit?" By the time you're at this point, no one can know the answer for sure, and you'll probably get a quick yes. ... I disagree and commit all the time. We recently greenlit a particular Amazon Studios original. I told the team my view: debatable whether it would be interesting enough, complicated to produce, the business terms aren't that good, and we have lots of other opportunities. They had a completely different opinion and wanted to go ahead. I wrote back right away with "I disagree and commit and hope it becomes the most watched thing we've ever made." Consider how much slower this decision cycle would have been if the team had actually had to convince me rather than simply get my commitment.*
>
> *Note what this example is not: it's not me thinking to myself "well, these guys are wrong and missing the point, but this isn't worth me chasing." It's a genuine disagreement of opinion, a candid expression of my view, a chance for the team to weigh my view, and a quick, sincere commitment to go their way. And given that this team has already brought home 11 Emmys, 6 Golden Globes, and 3 Oscars, I'm just glad they let me in the room at all!*

Bezos wisely recognized that if every team had to convince him and other executives that each decision was the right one, Amazon would quickly fall behind in meeting customer needs. Instead, Amazon executives made sure that each team fully owned its decisions and that the data and analysis used to make those decisions were rigorous.

Instilling Agency in Your Organization

One of my favorite examples of instilling agency in an organization stems from the use of employees' personal social media accounts to share corporate news and their work experiences. Most companies have a policy that only executives who have undergone media training are allowed to speak for the company. Imagine instead if employees had a sense of agency. What would they be inspired to share—or not? That opportunity and responsibility come from leaders and colleagues who give agency to their employees, not from formal organizational charts or process maps. Here are some best practices to give everyone in the organization that sense of ownership and the confidence to make bold decisions that can move your transformation efforts forward:

> **Demonstrate your trust in their judgment.** It's one thing to tell people they are in charge; it's another to *demonstrate* that you trust them to be in charge. When someone brings a problem to you, don't jump into problem-solving mode. Hold back and ask instead, "What do you think you should do to solve this problem?" or "What steps do you recommend?" You're building their confidence in their ability to address problems and to come to you as someone who can provide advice rather than as someone who will tell them what to do.

> **Shift ownership and authority in chunks.** If you give people ownership over a domain or a set of decisions overnight, they actually may not be ready to take it on. Instead, shift the responsibility to them over time—and tell them you are doing that.

First, ask them to come to the table with recommendations, then invite them to develop an action plan, and eventually have them make the decision. There is no easy shortcut to build ownership in people: shifting ownership requires intention, communication, and mentorship.

Forgive and learn from failure. If your organization is like most others, stigma and shame often follow failure. It's incumbent on you as a leader to acknowledge a failure but to also help the person who is accountable for it to move on. Conduct a healthy postmortem that focuses energy not on whom to blame but what everyone can learn and apply in the future. Codifying and sharing that learning broadly across the organization signals that failure must be turned into a learning opportunity and also makes it more acceptable to take risks. What should be clearly unacceptable is failure without learning—a wasted opportunity.

Simplify and clarify the decision-making framework. Take a look at your strategy and anticipate the kinds and levels of decisions that are going to have to change in order for that strategy to come to life. If you want to respond faster to customer concerns, who needs to approve those responses today? How should these decisions be made in the future? Systematically go through the strategy and identify where decision making is clogged, isn't clear, or doesn't exist. When everyone understands the limits of the decisions they own and where they can push boundaries, they are able to focus on getting the job done rather than worrying if they are stepping on toes. For example, if employees come across an unhappy customer, how much would they be able to spend to make things right? It's probably not thousands of dollars but can they spend $50?

Model the "disagree-and-commit" approach. As a leader, you make decisions all the time. Push out of your comfort zone and find an opportunity to support a team's decision, even though you don't agree with it. For example, if a group wants to test a new business model with a small group of customers or clients, support them even if you are not entirely sure the time is perfectly right for it.

"There are basically no companies that have good slow decisions. There are only companies that have good fast decisions."

—Larry Page, cofounder of Google and CEO of Alphabet

Clarify when disagreement is expected and when it's time to commit. One of the biggest fears about encouraging debate is that when discussions are over and a decision is made, bad feelings will remain between the parties. Bad feelings are more likely to arise if not all disagreements have been explored or when they surface after a decision has already been made. Make it very clear that there is a place and time for disagreement (e.g., at the start of a project), and take steps to encourage that all views and positions are shared. And also be clear that after this period of debate is over and a decision has been made, the expectation is that everyone will be 100 percent committed to that decision.

THE ACTION BELIEF: WORKING AT THE SPEED OF OPPORTUNITIES

Stuck cultures see change on the horizon and slow down or even actively try to avoid it. Flux cultures do just the opposite: they speed toward change because of the opportunities for growth that it represents.

The action belief is the sustained ability of an organization to recognize change opportunities and move quickly while executing at the highest levels. Flux cultures prefer action over inaction, taking risks rather than seeking certainty. They look at change and upheaval as normal and manageable and expect it to be part of their daily routine. They grow stronger, not weaker, with it. A bias for action allows organizations to constantly adapt themselves for the next hunt. It is embedded in every part of the organization, not reserved for a few anointed "innovators."

Stuck cultures often equate thorough analysis with excellence; they believe that being absolutely sure of the facts is the end goal. The problem is that they often justify doing more and more analysis to be sure they've weighed all their options, when in fact they are just putting off making a decision. This analysis paralysis leads to waiting for the perfect time to act, which, of course, never comes.

People in organizations that believe in action do just the opposite: they develop a skeleton of a plan and put a premium on acting quickly. That requires not being afraid to make decisions, even in the face of uncertainty. People in organizations who believe in action don't feel the need to do something right; they feel the need to do *something*.

This doesn't mean they are not afraid of failure, but they look at the data, calculate and accept the risk, and move forward into action. They know that the cost of not acting is far greater than the cost of making a mistake. They value *calculated* risk taking (note the emphasis on "calculated"); they make clear what risks would be unacceptable and then set people loose, saying, "Go for it!"

In my research, I've found that organizations with strong action beliefs exhibit the following behaviors:

They embrace "done is better than perfect." Flux organizations avoid the trap of trying to get something to be perfect before moving forward. They know that they can't make money from unlaunched products and services and that the longer they wait, the more likely it is that someone else will beat them to market. So they focus on making decisions and launching what some in the tech industry call a "minimally viable product" to see how customers use the product or service.

They test and fail their way to success. Organizations with a bias to action accept that making mistakes and failure are natural parts of the journey to success—that they are better off learning what works and doesn't work with customers than sitting in the lab and trying to figure it out.

They define next steps and deadlines. Organizations with a strong action belief are disciplined about always establishing clear next steps—and deadlines of when those steps will be completed so that decisions can be made.

These behaviors lead to one key capability: the ability to constantly try new things to figure out what actually works. If you instead focus on doing only what you know is going to work, you are leaving a lot of opportunities on the table.

Case Study: SNHU

Chapter 2 examined how Southern New Hampshire University (SNHU) made some big gulp decisions to become the largest provider of accredited college degrees in the world. Its leaders have also taken steps to act faster to capture opportunities that come their way.

On the morning of Friday, September 2, 2016, President Paul LeBlanc received a call from the US Department of Education notifying him that nearby Daniel Webster College was about to lose its accreditation and close because its parent, ITT, was declaring bankruptcy.[100] The department asked if SNHU would be interested in taking over Daniel Webster, allowing the students to continue their education. The problem was that SNHU had only six days to make and execute the decision before the accreditation was going to be pulled.

LeBlanc had restructured SNHU earlier that year for just this sort of opportunity, creating a "One SNHU" strategy that allowed greater cross-functional collaboration. By lunchtime the day of the notification, he had established a cross-functional team, and the next day, Saturday, the team was on the Daniel Webster campus. By Tuesday, September 6, SNHU had worked out an agreement with ITT that was announced the following day.

At any organization, let alone an educational institution, such an opportunity would likely have been referred up to a strategy committee, which would then have to loop in academic standards, and eventually go to the board for approval. That would have taken weeks, if not months. Instead, SNHU pulled all of the pre-identified people from the various departments and business units on to the team. LeBlanc also didn't have to worry about who "owned" the decision because everyone who wanted to participate was already involved.

Embracing a Bias for Action

How do you develop the ability to identify new opportunities and respond to them as quickly as SNHU did when it acquired Daniel Webster College? If your organization needs to increase its belief in action, consider adopting some of these best practices:

Increase and measure change capacity. Organizations with the action belief embrace the need to constantly change and evolve. They know that changing customer needs and conditions require that they constantly adjust. As a result, they prepare themselves emotionally. They also create structure and stability so rather than suffering from "change fatigue," they are energized to take action. In an effort to manage what matters, measure your organization's comfort level with change. Survey employees on how comfortable they are with change, and whether the prospect of change on the horizon makes them feel energized or weary. Conducting this audit will identify places where you need to focus your transformation efforts. Also when you are hiring, identify people who are already wired for change by asking questions that test for a bias for action.

Invest in and develop your employees' extrasensory skills. People don't develop a "spider sense" for detecting opportunities without practice and support. Encourage employees across all levels of the organization to develop their professional networks and share information about what is happening internally and externally, through crowd-sourcing or social networks and communities of experts. Make customer data and social listening tools accessible to employees so that they can spot and take action on market changes. Invest internally on platforms and training. It may be tempting to delay or cut spending on these areas, but they are mission critical to your ability to identify and shift into growth opportunities.

Define the decision field. There are two types of decisions that are typically made: ones that are easy to reverse and ones that are not. But even irreversible decisions can be okay as long as they don't completely debilitate the organization. If you want people to feel comfortable taking risks, you have to clearly define which mistakes and failures are tolerable and which aren't. Define the boundaries of the field that they are playing on, explaining that as long as they stay on their field, they are free to go anywhere the customer and market may take them. Similarly, make clear the definition of a "calculated" risk: What's the minimum needed to move forward?

Some organizations require only a tentative plan, a worst-case scenario analysis, and a few potential alternatives to pursue in case this action doesn't pan out.

"The way to get started is to quit talking and begin doing."

— Walt Disney, animator and entrepreneur

Force decisions and action with impossible deadlines. I've seen many organizations set deadlines based on when everyone feels they've gathered all of the data needed to make a decision. That's too slow! Instead, determine the minimal data needed to choose between option A and option B, figure out how long it will take to get that data, and make that the deadline. If your team is new at this, set an impossibly short deadline (hours and days, not days and week) to force them to come to the table with a decision, even if they are really uncomfortable with it. Over time, your team will get more comfortable making decisions with minimal analysis.

MOVING FORWARD

All of the research I've done points to one fundamental truth: the only way to change culture is to start working differently. Begin with a quick audit by asking people across the organization what's working well and what needs to improve. These discussions will give you insight into the underlying beliefs that make up your organization— and how consistently or inconsistently they are held across different departments, business units, or geographies. Compare your notes with the three beliefs of flux organizations, and you'll see the gaps that need to be addressed.

Then systematically go through the current beliefs of your organization and decide whether they—and the associated behaviors that reinforce them—are worth holding on to or if it's time to jettison them. Replace them with flux beliefs and behaviors that will enable you to confidently chase after your future customers and execute on your disruption strategy.

TAKEAWAYS

- ◆ Your disruptive transformation strategy can execute only as fast and as far as your culture allows it. To change your culture, you must shift the underlying beliefs and behaviors that define how work gets done.
- ◆ Organizations capable of driving disruptive transformation have three beliefs–openness, agency, and action—that enable them to thrive with disruption and change.
- ◆ You can start changing your culture by identifying the beliefs that hold you back and agreeing to not act on those beliefs anymore. To replace them, identify new beliefs and behaviors that your organization must adopt.

"Process drives culture, not the other way around, so you can't just change the culture, you have to change the system."

—Eric Reis, author of *Lean Startup* and *The Startup Way*

. . . .

CHAPTER 6

THE FLUX CULTURE OPERATING SYSTEM

THE PREVIOUS chapter examined how the three flux beliefs of being open, instilling agency in employees, and embracing a bias for action form the underpinnings of a disruption culture and how you can take the first step toward developing them. But just adopting these disruptive beliefs isn't enough to create and sustain disruptive transformation in your culture. You need to also hardwire those new beliefs into what I call the organization's operating system—its structure, formal and informal processes, rituals, symbols, and stories—so that the desired disruptive behaviors become the norm rather than the exception.

Without the disruption operating system, you can't coordinate and leverage the scale and power of your organization. It's one of the most ironic findings from my research: the most disruptive transformational organizations have strong and established operating systems, which appears to be in direct contradiction to disruption.

That's because most people think that "disruptive cultures" means that a lot of highly creative people do their own thing with little coordination or alignment. What I found at disruptive organizations instead was just the opposite: highly creative *and* accomplished people working *together* within clear structures and processes. By not having to worry about how to get work done, they could just focus on doing great work with each other.

If your operating system isn't tuned to your disruptive strategy and beliefs, it will drag your organization down. Uncertainty about reporting structures and decision-making processes results in politics; crucial data remain locked in silos; and stories of heroic measures echo of past glories rather than reflect existing realities. Instead of moving the organization forward, the operating system grinds to a halt. One executive I worked with described running disruptive transformation initiatives like pushing a huge boulder up the hill. The team was suffering "change fatigue," feeling they had been in a constant state of fighting for monumental change in the organization with not much to show for their efforts. They were exhausted and demoralized.

But when I talk with disruptive organizations about their operating systems, they describe their transformation efforts differently. Yes, it's hard to create disruption, but it doesn't *stay* hard. At some point, the structure, routines, and process kick in, and it actually gets easier, requiring less effort to sustain the new way of working.

A cohesive, stable operating system ensures that everyone in the organization is aligned with the vision, strategy, and beliefs before taking off. Like a well-tuned race car, your culture operating system works together as the engine that drives the organization faster down the road. By having to spend less effort on each disruptive initiative, fatigue is less likely to set in. And without that fatigue, a flux organization is able to take on more disruptive change. It's the epitome of the disruption flywheel.

MICROSOFT HITS THE REFRESH BUTTON

In 2011, Satya Nadella was made deeply uncomfortable by something he saw on the Web. A programmer at Google, Manu Cornet, had published a cartoon meant to humorously show the many ways top tech companies are organized.[101] The cartoon featured six illustrations of organizational structures at companies like Amazon and Apple.

But the one that illustrated Microsoft's structure stood out: it depicted multiple divisions pointing guns at each other.

At the time, Nadella knew that Microsoft was not headed in the right direction. "After years of outdistancing all of our competitors, something was changing and not for the better. Innovation was being replaced by bureaucracy. Teamwork was being replaced by internal politics. We were falling behind," he writes in his book, *Hit Refresh*.[102] The cartoon was a painful reminder of how deeply its culture had changed for the worst. "The humorist message was impossible to ignore," he writes. "As a 24-year veteran of Microsoft, a consummate insider, the caricature really bothered me. But what upset me more was that our own people just accepted it."

Nadella recognized that in order to turn Microsoft around, he had to get the company to think and work differently. He made culture change his number one priority and promoted the concept of having empathy—for customer, employees, partners— as the centerpiece belief of the new Microsoft culture. In 2015, Microsoft reinforced the new strategy and culture by reorganizing these previously rival business units into the same groups (e.g., putting Windows software and devices into the same group).[103]

Getting a company to think and work differently, as Microsoft did, requires an enormous amount of discipline. Each person in the organization must be willing to give up some freedom and adhere to guidelines and guardrails that ensure clarity, consistency, and stability. In a world fraught with great uncertainty, knowing what *isn't* going to change gives people confidence that the foundation isn't going to shift beneath them.

At the same time, everyone must commit themselves to rigorously work toward achieving high standards of execution. Knowing that high standards are being set and met by everyone in the organization ensures that everyone is pulling their own weight. The more uncertainty you deal with in your day-to-day work, the more order, clarity, and foundational structure you need in other areas.

I've seen many organizations undertake disruptive transformations but focus primarily on the strategy elements and ignore or defer addressing these issues until it's too late. You can't simply snap your fingers, declare yourself a disruptive organization, and expect that everyone will know what that means on an operational level. Ensuring alignment consumes time, energy, and resources; it is not something taken for granted. Yes, it can be mind-numbingly boring to prepare RACI (Create a Responsibility Assignment Matrix) charts or lay out a new process. It may feel silly creating a new recognition ritual. But it is all essential to have a well-developed operating system that can support disruptive growth.

> "Talent without discipline is like an octopus on roller skates. There's plenty of movement, but you never know if it's going to be forward, backwards, or sideways."
>
> – H. Jackson Brown Jr., *Life's Little Instruction Book*

The beauty of focusing on your culture operating system is that it allows you to modify elements to directly addressing disorderly behaviors. For example, one sales team leader I knew was frustrated that the sales team was not following a new positioning for the company. It turned out that a new value proposition was being foisted on the salespeople every six months. The team had no confidence that leadership knew what they were doing, so why change how they operated if it was just going to change again? They kept doing things the same way, hoping that no one would notice.

In another organization I worked with, a star player suffered no consequences for not hitting some basic commitments, quarter after quarter. The result was that the other team members started slacking off as well, betting that they also wouldn't suffer the consequences. The management team knew this was a problem, but didn't have the backbone to demand that the star player fall in line out of fear that he would leave and take his top accounts with him.

Do these situations sound familiar? You can't move fast and chase after your future customers when you are still struggling with executing the basics of serving your customers today. A well-thought-out and intentional operating system creates a sense of order that brings three foundational benefits to your organization:

1. Organizations with a strong disruptive operating system build better products and services for customers because you are aligned and working on the same thing.

2. High-performing people are drawn to well-run companies, which helps with recruiting and retention.

3. Organizations with a strong process can cycle faster through disruption because they have a strong foundation that doesn't need to change.

I recently worked with an organization that pulled together in the face of a competitive threat, identified a new manufacturing process, and pushed new products into the market quickly. A success! "That was two years ago, and we are still recovering!" its chief strategy officer admitted. The process nearly destroyed them because it was so difficult to reestablish order. I've found that the fastest-moving companies avoid this kind of burnout by not making big bets. Instead, they make many tiny bets very quickly and return to a state of order before going through another cycle of stretching. Disruptive organizations are like athletes: they train consistently, stretching each time to push capabilities a little further.

Recovery is as important a part of training as exertion. Just as athletes systematically schedule time for their bodies to rebuild, organizations need to do so as well. Without that pause to recover and recenter, your organization risks pushing too far too quickly and having to step back to make up for mistakes that might otherwise have been avoided. Because power relationships are constantly shifted and rewritten during times of disruptive change, an organization needs time to figure out where everyone is and how everyone is going to move forward *together* before it can proceed. It's counterintuitive: you have to slow down to go fast.

In this chapter, I go into greater detail on how disruptive organizations take the time to define their flux culture by systematically developing and then relying on the three cultural elements that comprise an organization's operating system to help them weather and thrive with disruption: structure, processes, and lore (see Figure 6.1):

Structure. Structure defines the power relationships in the workplace, as well as the physical proximity of people to each other. In an increasingly digital and remote workplace, structure takes on even more importance in defining when and how people work with each other.

Processes. Processes include anything that can be captured and written down as repeatable steps or a policy that guides the development of a process. Examples range from the strategic planning process and how investments are prioritized to minutiae like how meetings are run or feedback is given.

Lore. According to the *Oxford Dictionary*, lore is "a body of traditions and knowledge on a subject or held by a particular group, typically passed from person to person by word of mouth."[104] These are the stories, symbols, rituals, and traditions that people share with each other. They become a type of shorthand for colleagues to confirm with each other that they are together, fighting the same fight. More important, they reflect the emotional bonds of trust that smooths the path to change.

Fig. 6.1 The Culture Operating Model

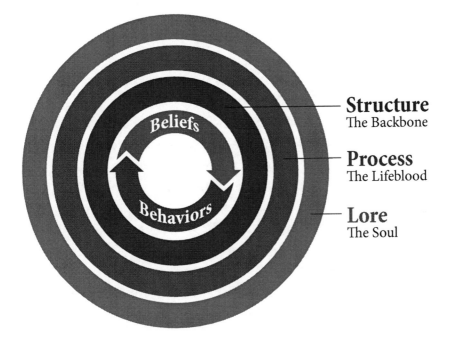

Structure
The Backbone

Process
The Lifeblood

Lore
The Soul

STRUCTURE: THE BACKBONE OF YOUR OPERATING MODEL

The structure of departments and business units plays an important role in organizations because it makes clear how information and decision making flow throughout the organization. People who need to work frequently with each other logically should sit figuratively and literally next to each other in the organizational structure.

In stable times, structure provides focus and accountability, creating efficiencies to get you to the next level of productivity. The focus is on execution and delivering on short-term business goals. What disruptive organizations do exceedingly well is that they also build flexibility into the structure to support chasing after new opportunities to serve future customers. They have some degree of separation between the innovation part and the core of the organization, allowing disruptive change to find its own footing. And they also have some level of connection to the core that allows them to realize synergies in resources, expertise, and the marketplace.

But most traditional organizations separate the innovation part of the organization from the core—and that is their biggest mistake. During times of flux and change, those silos become a handicap because you need to build windows and bridges between those entities to create new products that meet new customer needs. With the time between periods of constancy and change decreasing, traditional organizational hierarchies are not cutting it. While most organization shave formal organizational charts, the way work actually gets done looks completely different (see Figure 6.2).

There are data to back this up. The annual Katzenbach Center Global Culture Survey found that only 58 percent of senior leaders (the C-suite and board members) agree or strongly agree that the formal organization chart reflects how things get done.[105] Worse, only 45 percent of nonmanagement employees agree that this is true.

The disconnect between formal organizational structures and the way work really gets done is the reason organizations go through so many reorganizations. They are an attempt to close the gap between what's on paper and how work in fact gets done.

In almost every case, organizations believe that moving the boxes around on the chart will shift the culture or that the new structure will result in better ways to execute their objectives.

It doesn't work that way. Organizational change works when you identify the beliefs and behaviors you want to change, and then create new structures to reinforce those new beliefs and behaviors.

Fig. 6.2 Traditional Organization Charts Don't Reflect How Work Really Gets Done

Traditional organization chart

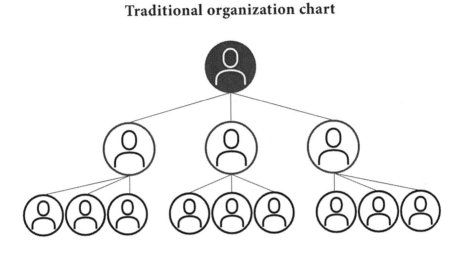

How work actually gets done

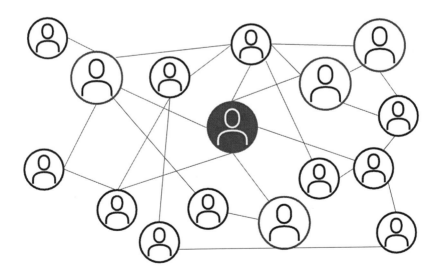

Going Agile at ING Bank

ING, a retail bank in the Netherlands, is a great example of an organization that grounded its new organizational structure on the beliefs and behaviors it wanted to change. ING could see the banking industry was undergoing seismic changes and that to survive, they would have to work in a new way: they would have to become more agile. "The key was getting IT people and businesspeople together on one team where they could work independently and think about a product, build it, and take it to market as independently as possible," explained Nick Jue, ING's CEO in the Netherlands at the time.[106]

To kick-start the transformation, the leadership team studied companies like Google, Netflix, Spotify, and Zappos that had been working in agile teams for years. The result was a deep understanding of the benefits of agility. When the bank rolled out an announcement in November 2014 about the coming structural changes, its leaders were prepared to communicate the "why" and "what" driving the initiative: to shorten the time to market to improve customer experience and improve the bank's digital capabilities. Employees were excited that they were joining the ranks of companies like Netflix and Google.

In the ensuing weeks, the focus shifted to the "how," which included breaking down departments and re-forming into small teams and letting employees know what it would mean for each of them personally. The benefit of separating the "why" and "what" from the "how" was that everyone understood why the bank had to make this change, even if they didn't yet completely understand just how radically different the new "how" would be.

In spring 2015, the transition began, starting with the leadership team at the level right under the ING Netherlands executive team. The employees had to reapply for new positions. When positions were not filled with the same people—employees and leaders who were seen as experts on a topic and had done that job for years—it was a real wake-up call for everyone in the company. The selection process didn't focus just on employees' knowledge and experience. It also took into account their mindsets and behaviors aligned with the "Orange Code," the company's new values (see Figure 6.3).

Fig. 6.3 ING's Orange Code

The Orange Code
Our behaviours

You take it on and make it happen

You take responsibility for getting it done, for keeping your promises, for the consequences of your actions

You delegate to motivate others, maintain momentum and create impact

You ask actively for help and feedback. Your colleagues will help you succeed if you let them

You speak up - crediting good work and having the courage to confront poor performance

You help others to be successful

You collaborate - putting personal agendas aside to achieve the goals that matter to ING

You listen - investing in others, irrespective of status, background or opinion

You contribute across business lines and bring in people from outside your area

You trust the intention and expertise of others

You are always a step ahead

You challenge conventions, complexity and your own assumptions, but only when you are prepared to be part of the solution

You bring change by adapting quickly when the situation calls for a new approach

You invent and simplify - if it doesn't work, you reinvent it. If it does work, you make it better

You are courageous - admitting and learning from mistakes by being open about them

Source: ING Bank

159

The goal of this rehiring process was to identify people who would thrive in the new way of working, which was going to be radically different from the old ING Netherlands. When the selection process was finished three months later, 25 percent of the headquarters staff were not rehired. In addition, most managers and directors no longer had their titles; they were now organized into a structure made up of tribes, squads, and chapters (see Figure 6.4).

Fig. 6.4 Organizational Structure at ING Netherlands

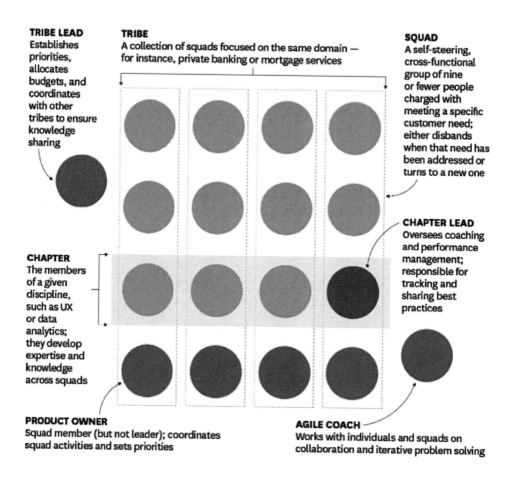

Source: "One Bank's Agile Team Experiment," Harvard Business Review, March-April 2018

To the outsider, this new organizational structure appears to be designed to maximize mayhem rather than streamline operations. And as the bank initially prioritized setting up autonomous, self-steering squads and tribes, partially this was indeed the case. In short order, ING instituted the Quarterly Business Review (QBR), modeled after Netflix's. Each quarter, tribe leads gather to review what everyone is working on and align their efforts to the bank's priorities.

While the organizational structure is a big part of ING's transformation, there is an underlying and more important shift happening at the bank. "When we start talking about agile transformations, we talk about tribes and squads but that really is not the big change," explains Gijs Valbracht, agile coach at ING, in a Harvard Business School case study. [107] "The big change is on the mindset part: Why do we want to collaborate in the organization?" That "why"—greater flexibility and agility to chase after new customers—is crucial.

How to Design a Disruptive Organizational Structure

The ING Netherlands case study is a great example of an organization committed to moving to an organizational structure that supports disruption. But agile teams are not the only structure that can do this. There is no perfect organization structure for disruptive transformation. There is only the perfect one for *your* strategy and *your* organization at this particular time. Here are a few best practices to help you get started with your own organizational transformation:

Understand and accept the truth about your organization. Conduct a close audit of your organization. Dig down to find where the disconnects are between your organizational structure and how work really gets done. This is also an opportunity to uncover where the real power brokers reside in the organization. You'll likely find that they are not necessarily those with a big title but, rather, individual contributors with deep networks throughout the organization. I guarantee you that uncomfortable truths will surface quickly. Accept them and plan how the future organizational structure will take that reality into account while supporting the future desired state.

Organize around future customers, not products or functions. Most organizations claim to be customer focused. But when customers are truly at the center of your business, everything proceeds from an organizing principle based on answering this simple question: What's best for them? Instead of structuring your organization around functional departments or product groups, structure it around current and future customer needs. For example, Intermountain Healthcare, the largest health care provider and insurer in Utah, moved from a geographic-defined structure into a system-wide structure with two main groups, a Community Care group focused on making sure people stay healthy and a Specialty Care group to serve patients who require hospitalization or specialist procedures.[108] The processes and metrics are different for these two care groups and align with the needs of their very different patients.

Map out critical relationships. What kind of new power relationships need to be formed to execute your transformation strategy? Map out where the most important, frequent, and difficult connections must be made and engineer that relationship into reality with your structure. One organization I know combined two teams, technology and strategy, that frequently encountered disconnects because they didn't speak the same language. By having them report into the same organization and also sit literally next to each other, they started to bridge the gap and form a common understanding.

Break windows between silos. One challenge I frequently hear is that departments and business units harden into silos that defy reorganization. An approach that I've seen work at companies is not to aim for breaking down silos completely. Instead, punch data and communication "windows" between them to enable people to *see* each other and work together from within those silos. The key is to know where to make the windows and how big to make them so that they support a specific business objective. For example, one business-to-business organization connected the marketing and sales department by linking social media engagement data from marketing campaigns into customer profiles that sales used. With that "data window" in place, account-based teams from marketing and sales collaborated to create customized marketing content for each customer based on where it was in the sales cycle.

Reflect how work gets done in both physical and digital workspaces. When ING Netherlands shifted its entire headquarters to an agile organizational model, all employees attended a day-long kick-off in a nearby stadium and returned the next workday to a completely redesigned office space created to support multidisciplinary agile teams. Use the physical workspace to create the new relationships you want, from informal "collision" points in hallways to no offices for executives to encourage openness and access. Also examine how digital collaboration is (or isn't) happening, and design digital workspaces that can support new working relationship with little friction. For example, set up a collaboration space where marketing, sales, and service operations regularly connect with product development to share frontline customer feedback.

Build flexibility into your organizational design to minimize disruptive restructuring. Given that changes are the norm when you pursue a disruptive growth strategy, you must anticipate where flexibility is needed in your organizational structure and build that into the design. For example, with technology changing so quickly, IT needs to both centralize expertise for a new technology like AI but also anticipate that as it matures, expertise will need to migrate and develop in business units. Similarly, as customer segments ebb and flow, being able to move people around seamlessly becomes a competitive advantage.

PROCESSES: THE LIFEBLOOD OF THE ORGANIZATION

Processes—from formal ones like strategic planning and hiring, to informal processes like meeting protocols and how feedback is given and accepted—are literally the blood that flows throughout your organization. If they flow well, you feel strong, capable of running long and hard. If processes don't work, it's like having a knot in your muscle— you can still move but at a limping pace. Good processes provide clarity and certainty around execution, remove doubt, and allow you to spend your time focused on being creative and solving problems.

But good processes morph quickly into bad ones when they are adopted to accomplish new tasks created by a disruptive growth strategy. When processes don't get updated to match the evolution of how work is changing, a disconnect follows.

Let's take a look at a few formal and informal processes that disruptive organizations use to illustrate how they help them be more customer focused and also move faster.

Approving New Initiatives at Amazon

At the start of every project at Amazon, the team writes a one-page press release from the future, describing what problem the proposed product or service will solve along with six pages of FAQs that lay out details about how customers will use it.[109] The team might spend weeks creating and refining that press release, but by the end of the exercise, they walk away with a crisp and clear explanation of how the project will help customers. This approach forms the innovation infrastructure for Amazon—every proposal for a new product or service follows this format. It ingrains the leadership principle "Be customer obsessed" into the innovation process by starting with the end customer experience and working backward to today.

The Global Process to Drive Innovation at Huawei

One of the best examples of process driving disruptive transformation is Huawei, the Chinese Internet and telecommunications giant founded in 1987 by Ren Zhengfei, a former military engineer.[110] The company grew from its humble beginning manufacturing phone switches into the largest Internet and communications company in the world, with $108.5 billion in sales in 2018.[111] Huawei is the second biggest maker of mobile handsets (behind Samsung and just ahead of Apple) and has seen average compound revenue growth of 21 percent since 2007. That's 21 percent average growth over eleven years.[112]

With operations in more than 170 countries and 180,000 employees from 161 countries, Huawei is a sprawling, diverse operation. Yet I found it to be surprisingly nimble. I attribute much of its growth over these past eleven years to its culture and an underlying belief in and adherence to process. For example, Huawei has 80,000 employees working on some type of research and development in its fourteen innovation centers around the world. "R&D is centrally managed so we know the requirements from different markets," explained Joy Tan, president of global media and communications at Huawei.[113] "We can then prioritize requirements that will apply to the most markets." Scientists and engineers who travel between the company's innovation centers find that the same protocols are followed in all of them, making it easy to move, work, and share their research globally. As a result, any customer can benefit almost immediately from something happening on the other side of the world.

From Annual to Quarterly Strategic Planning Process at Voicea

In most organizations, the strategic planning process happens on a fixed yearly cycle. The outcome of this annual process is a well-documented, single point of view of what the future will look like—for example, that so many million customers will have smartphones or that machine learning and the Internet of things will roll out at a certain rate. The resulting strategic plan is what the organization should do if *all* of these assumptions are true.

Inevitably, a funny thing happens along the way: those assumptions don't come true or, more likely, the rate at which they come to be speed up or slow down. Although you have better information to feed and refine your assumption about how the world will be in the future, you can't make changes to your strategic plan because it is "locked and loaded" for the next year. This brittle strategy fails to take into account that the future might be radically different from what you predicted. It also fails to develop the ability to shift course quickly in case assumptions shift.

My strong belief is that every organization should be engaging in quarterly, not yearly, strategic planning reviews, scanning the landscape and the horizon for changes. Then its leaders should reexamine the underlying assumptions that drive their strategy and make changes accordingly. Voicea, a voice collaboration platform, is one of the fast-growing start-ups that conduct such quarterly strategic planning. Its founder, Omar Tawakol, a veteran entrepreneur who sold his previous company, BlueKai, to Oracle, explains, "If you're experiencing a 10X inflexion every four to five months it's senseless to do a year strategy. The dynamic changes too quickly."[114]

In the ninth week of each quarter, Tawakol begins the strategy planning process, sending his initial thoughts about how he sees the customer priorities and the surrounding ecosystem changing to his leadership team. Over the next four weeks, those leaders do a bottom-up review and share information, data, and opinions back and forth via digital collaboration platforms, updating scenarios and metrics and narrowing options. Leadership holds a day-long off-site meeting to ensure alignment across all of their priorities. The outcomes are then shared at a quarterly kick-off meeting with the company.

Looking back at his quarterly strategy plans, Tawakol pointed out how strategy shifted significantly between Q2 and Q3 in 2018 because they became more confident that their product was strong enough to drive viral sign-ups. They thus made virality a strategic priority and a key metric to track. "We're still in the mode where we try to keep a longer-term view on the strategy," Tawakol explained. "But we're willing to revisit what the emphasis is every quarter."

This may seem like overkill if your industry doesn't appear to be changing. But just because you and your competitors aren't changing doesn't mean that your customers and your ecosystem are standing still. The quarterly strategy planning process becomes a way to hardwire an understanding of the future customer deeply into one of the core processes of your organization.

Redefining Success and Failure in the Investment Review Process at Schibsted

The investment process—and, by association, product development—in status quo companies is designed to minimize risk and push incremental optimizations forward. But even when organizations make the commitment to transform and disrupt, I find that they throw a lot of money at too many poorly designed and executed initiatives.

One organization I worked with had fifteen major initiatives, all with eighteen- to twenty-four-month execution time lines. Compare that to a struggling start-up that can afford to focus on one thing and do only that one thing well. When your resources are constrained as theirs are, you become good at designing and executing initiatives, but also at killing them off.

While most organizations have an evaluation process with specific milestones to hit, they lack the discipline to adhere to the process. They always find extenuating circumstances to blame—for example, resources weren't available. Whatever the excuse, the result is the same: the organization continues to throw valuable resources and talent at a floundering initiative because it's easier to do that than to pay the political price of shutting down someone's pet project. Underlying this inability to call it quits is a stigma associated with failure. Examining how definitions of success and failure stymie the decision-making process around your investments and divestments is crucial.

That was the situation in which the newspaper company Schibsted found itself during the early 2000s as the organization was moving into the online classifieds space. In the past, shutting down an initiative was seen as the failure of a manager or division, so executives fought hard to keep their faltering efforts alive. A shift in this mindset at Schibsted happened when the bursting of the dot-com bubble brought with it a renewed sense to rein in investments.[115]

In one case, despite having made significant investment in online classifieds in Portugal, heavy competition from the local player backed by Naspers, South Africa technology investment meant Schibsted would face a protracted battle for years. Instead, it decided to redeploy those resources into other markets. But leadership made clear that the decision to abandon the Portuguese market was made because of market forces, not because of failure on the part of the Portuguese leadership or organization. "All of these things gave us a way of institutionalizing killing our babies or our darlings when we had to," the former chief strategy officer, Sverre Munck, recalled. "It took us almost ten years to change that mindset. We could have done it much sooner if we had been more aware of how important it was to our success."

Informal Meeting Protocols Set Clear Expectations at Google

Informal processes can also be habits practiced by teams and individuals. Consider how meetings work at Google.[116] They begin right on time and end a little early so that people can get to their next meetings on time. When they sit down at the meeting table, something curious happens: everyone puts their laptops and phones *away*. Only one person takes notes, which are then made available for everyone to review. Everyone is 100 percent present and focused on the discussion, not multitasking on email. And there's a physical clock counting down the time.

As the meeting draws to a close, the people using the room next gather in the hall and come in at the appointed time, starting their meeting regardless of whether people from the previous meeting are still in the room! Google is a sprawling international enterprise with almost 100,000 employees. Having a consistent, familiar process for meetings creates the connective tissue for people from all corners of the organization working together.

Marrying Formal and Informal Processes to Drive Strategy Alignment at Intermountain Healthcare

Intermountain Healthcare in Utah has a process to ensure daily alignment against strategic goals across its 39,000 employees. Dan Liljenquist, senior vice president and chief strategy officer, said, "We have huddles every day across our teams that escalate up issues that we're trying to watch."[117]

Those huddles are quick meetings that focus on the organization's five fundamentals of care: safety, quality, patient experience, access, and stewardship. They can happen in informal settings, from a nursing station on a hospital floor to a single doctor's office. "We hardwire in opportunities to give additional clarity and to receive feedback every day," Liljenquist explains. "We communicate down and up simultaneously with thousands of huddles across the organization that end up in a single bidirectional reporting flow to facilitate communication."

Intermountain Healthcare's huddle process is a marrying of just enough formal and informal process to ensure there is a continual flow of information; it is not a technology platform. "We've been doing this for over three years," Liljenquist explained, "And it's given us this situational awareness that allowed us to try some of our larger bets."

How to Design Disruptive Processes

It's quite a conundrum: On one hand, you need clear and consistent processes to ensure that everyone is aligned without squelching disruptive thinking and behaviors. On the other hand, you need those processes to change frequently to reflect how the work being done is changing. It feels like an impossible task, but it isn't if you accept change as a norm: that processes will always be under development. Here are a few ways to get started in identifying and putting in place smooth processes for your disruptive culture operating system:

Demonstrate the benefits of the processes early on. Simply telling people that order is needed won't work; you'll have to explain why processes will support your disruptive transformation. There are two key benefits of processes: your organization will build better products and services for your customers, and it will attract high-performing people. Find a way to demonstrate how adhering to process can move things forward faster rather than slow things down. One example is having better meetings: starting on time with clear agendas, outcomes, and accountability. Planning great meetings takes more time, but if the outcomes include better, faster results, everyone will see the benefits and (I hope!) emulate this new behavior.

Clarify what is open to changing—and what isn't. Early on in Facebook's history, the motto, "Move fast and break things," made a lot of sense. But as the company grew, it morphed into, "Move fast with stable infrastructure."[118] It may not be as catchy, but Facebook had to deal with the reality that some things were simply not breakable. Audit your organization for instances when your team slows down because they are unsure if they have permission to change how they go about doing their work. Make those areas your top priority for establishing process and clarity.

Partner with disciplined leaders. If you lean more toward being an agile visionary rather than a consistent operator, find disciplined, methodical, and structured people to be your deputy or mentor. Take note of their behaviors and habits and find ways to incorporate them into your own leadership practices. In particular, watch how they use tools like dashboards and scorecards to identify early warning signs of processes that are out of whack.

Create accountability for consistently high standards. By being clear about "what good looks like," you are defining the parameters of great performance. One of Amazon's leadership principle is "insist on high standards."[119] It delivers on this principle by having a set of service-level agreements for everything from delivering packages to individual performance. But standards alone aren't enough; you also need the grit to follow through with consequences if they are not met. Consistency is everything when it comes to establishing process.

LORE: THE SOUL OF THE ORGANIZATION

If organizational structure is the spine and process the lifeblood of culture, then lore is its soul. Rituals, symbols, and stories remind and connect everyone—from executives and employees to partners and customers—about what is important and valued in the organization. Lore builds connection and trust among employees through repeated experiences that have a shared meaning. It's the telling and retelling of the lore—its repetition and consistency—that creates culture.

Aligning your company's lore with the objectives and values of its disruptive growth strategy can help create and sustain a flux culture. But just as easily, lore can harden into undesirable beliefs and calcify into undesirable behaviors. For example, one organization had a ritual of giving an employee-of-the-month award to spur friendly competition among team members. But it soon became clear that the award went to the person who talked the most with the key executive.

Backstabbing and gossip became more frequent as employees tried to make others look bad as a way to eliminate the competition. Similarly, elevating stories of "road warriors" who travel for twenty days out of the month or work eighty hours a week can set expectations that excessive time at spent at work is valued over results.

If you want to create disruptive transformation, you need to understand your company's lore and which of its elements—rituals, symbols, and stories—are holding back your culture. Then you must systematically and, intentionally replace them with new rituals, symbols, and hero stories.

Rituals

Rituals are a set of specific things that we always do at a particular time or milestone. For example, fans of the University of Alabama football team greet or acknowledge each other with a simple "Roll Tide!" a division starts every quarterly meeting by inviting employees to share what they are excited about at work, or an organization holds a drinks event every time they meet a product delivery date.

The experience of a ritual develops a shared identity, creating a sense of belonging and trust in the tribe and thereby reducing stress and anxiety and stimulating energy and emotions in participants. Ritual thus becomes a vital component of disruptive change because it alleviates some of the unpredictability and creates connection and a sense of belonging.

One of the best examples of the role of rituals is the haka, a Maori posture dance that the New Zealand rugby team performs before matches.[120] Research shows that besides being a vehicle for players to express pride in their team and heritage, the haka triggers a sense of flow, reducing players' anxiety and increasing focus.

Southwest Airlines is another organization that leans on rituals to reinforce its values of Warrior Spirit, Servant's Heart, and of course, "Fun-LUVing Attitude." Spirit parties, Southwest rallies, and anniversary celebrations all bring employees together to celebrate and build the Southwest culture. Halloween, for example, is a *really* big deal at Southwest Airlines, with employees from baggage handlers to the CEO dressing up in costume. Even CEO Gary Kelly participates.[121] And rituals like the CEO and president meeting with every new pilot imparts the company's commitment to passenger safety and experience.[122]

Here are a few examples of how new rituals shifted an organization's beliefs and values:

- When Howard Schultz returned as CEO of Starbucks in 2008, his top priority was to take the company back to its roots: serving quality coffee. One new ritual he created was that every newly hired employee does a tasting of the store manager's favorite coffees. The manager shares the story of where and how the coffee is grown, how it's brewed, and why he or she loves it so much. The experience connects both the manager and the new person not only to Starbuck's core value but also to each other.[123]

- LinkedIn is about engaging with and building professional networks. It realized that parents are often overlooked as a source of support and advice. So it sponsors a "Bring In Your Parents" day, a global company event designed to say "thank you" to the support parents have given LinkedIn employees and to help them understand what their children do.[124] The event is both in-person and virtual and supported with rich tool kits so that any team can create its own unique experience for parents and employees.

- Former Dun & Bradstreet CEO Jeff Stibel wanted to rewire how the organization thought about failure by adopting a "growth mindset" to look at mistakes as temporary setbacks that unveiled new paths to the objective. He quietly returned to his office one night and created a "failure wall," using a marker to write some of his biggest failures on the wall for everyone to see. People were encouraged to write their biggest failures on the wall too, include their learnings and to sign their name.[125] "It allowed us to talk about mistakes," Stibel wrote in a blog post. "It gave us an easy way to propose a risky idea: 'This might end up on the failure wall, but what if we ...'"

What kind of ritual can you create in your organization to connect your people to each other and their shared purpose? The more unique, insider, and frankly bizarre the ritual, the better. It's the power of the secret handshake to create and sustain a bond and create a sense of belonging. But it can also be as simple as bringing in coffee and doughnuts once a week and setting aside time to sit and connect. The key is that everyone participates, and it's done with consistency. It's the actual experience of the ritual that creates meaning.

Symbols

Symbols stand as silent sentinels, reminding us of common beliefs. One of my favorite examples of symbols comes from Oxo, the maker of well-designed housewares. Founder Sam Farber's wife, who has arthritis, was having trouble peeling potatoes, so he designed a better peeler. He went on to found Oxo, which is dedicated to making innovative products that make everyday living easier. On one wall of Oxo's New York City headquarters cafeteria hang over 100 gloves that employees found discarded throughout the city (see Figure 6.5).[126] The Glove Wall is there as a reminder for employees to have empathy for the many different types of hands that must use their products.

Similarly, new employees at SNHU's online learning division sign a mission statement mounted on a wall near their desk (see Figure 6.6). Multiple times a day, they pass that sign, their eyes drifting to their signature, and it serves as a symbol and reminder of their personal commitment to the mission.

Fig. 6.5 Oxo's Glove Wall in Its New York City Headquarters

Source: Oxo.

Fig. 6.6 SNHU's Mission with Employee Signatures

Source: SNHU.

And at Amazon, Jeff Bezos named the headquarters office building "Day 1," a phrase that comes from his very first shareholder letter where he laid out that to stay fresh and relevant to customers, Amazon must live every day as if it is Day 1 of the Internet (see Figure 6.7).[127] As employees walk by the building's sign every morning, they are reminded to live Day 1 that day.

Fig. 6.7 Entrance to Amazon's Day 1 Office Building

Source: GeekWire Photo / Kurt Schlosser.

Not all symbols are physical embodiments. When Electrolux, a Swedish manufacturer of home appliances, embarked on a digital transformation that refocused the company on its customers, it had to rethink the customer journey for a product category where the time between purchases is measured in years, if not decades. By focusing on how the appliance was used over the years, the company began thinking about the customer experience from a completely different perspective and created a symbol (see Figure 6.8) as a shorthand for it. That symbol began appearing on all of its internal documents and is embedded in its presentation templates. It shows up frequently during training sessions designed to create a culture of experience innovation among the top innovators across the company.[128]

Fig. 6.8 Electrolux's Symbol for the Customer Journey

Source: Electrolux.

Stories

Stories are a powerful agent of change because they are easy to tell, share, and remember. They can also change perceptions and create energy as they engage our emotions. And stories are not adversarial and nonhierarchical; they can come from anywhere.

Of course, simply telling a story about the future isn't enough to shape organizational culture As a rhetorical device, it can be easily dismissed. "Burning platform" stories may galvanize action in the moment, but they generate inherently negative reactions: once the fear goes away, the impetus for change dissipates with it.[129] Moreover, stories from the past can unintentionally anchor us there.

The most powerful type of story to shape organizational culture is what I call "hero springboard" stories. It features a single protagonist as the hero who overcomes a problem to reach victory. In these stories, listeners can see themselves as heroes in their own narratives. They act as a springboard as listeners begin to imagine what the future could be if they acted in a similar way as the hero in the story.

One organization that uses story extensively is Huawei. I've gotten to know Huawei quite a bit over the past few years, including a visit to its headquarters in Shenzhen. First and foremost, it is a company focused on going the extra mile, literally, to serve customers. And hero stories that reinforce that customer-first mindset abound: the engineer who transported telecom equipment on a mule on dirt roads across Uzbekistan; the employee who waited outside an office for three days to get a meeting with a manager; even of its founder, Ren Zhengfei, taking taxis instead of private cars so that he can express humility.

One of the best stories I heard was about an account manager who was undercut by the competition to the point where he felt that lowering the price further would compromise the quality of the solution. He went back to the customer, apologized for not being able to meet the price demands, and explained that Huawei would never do something that would be bad for the customer. Fully expecting that he had lost the deal, he left, dejected. The next day, the customer called to give him the deal. The telling and retelling of that story reinforces that Huawei will put customers first even if it means financial setbacks.

These hero stories all have the same purpose: to remind Huawei's sprawling, diverse organizational members of their personal role in living the company's core values. Their power is not the story itself, but the fact that they inspire behaviors. And because hero stories can come from anywhere in the organization—customer success, an employee overcoming obstacles, an ingenious solution born out of need—they are a testament to how every person in your organization's ecosystem can participate in the creation of its lore.

"To change something, build a new model that makes the existing model obsolete."

—R. Buckminster Fuller, architect and designer of geodesic domes

Using Lore to Create Flux Cultures

Lore works great if it aligns with your disruption strategy and the other two elements of culture. But it fails when it becomes a defense of the status quo, used to justify clinging to the past. In particular, stories that glorify long-held beliefs, such as prioritizing a particular set of customers, can block exploring new customers. I once worked for a firm where 70 percent of its business came from existing large customers, and all of the hero stories centered on work done for a few select customers from the distant past. That left little room for new customer stories to surface and communicate a desire to go after new opportunities. In such circumstances, organizations must systematically and intentionally create and spread new lore that replaces the outmoded one.

I often see organizations jumping too quickly to create rituals, symbols, and stories. A CEO mandate to change the culture inevitably results in the creation of lots of posters, memos, and day-long workshops. This is what I call "innovation theater," where we play at making disruptive change but little happens. Please spare your organization this charade and instead focus on creating meaningful lore.

To effectively change your lore, you have to know what lore already exists in your organization: the good, the bad, and the downright ugly. By cataloging existing rituals, symbols, and stories, you can identify which ones align with the new beliefs of your disruptive strategy and which ones you need to replace with new ones. Here are a few ways to conduct a "lore audit":

Take new hires out to lunch. Within the first month of their joining the organization, ask them what their experience has been like. What did they find surprising about the organization? What unspoken rules did they encounter? Which makes sense? Which do they find don't fit what they expected? Those fresh eyes are invaluable in giving you feedback on what your culture actually looks like.

Uncover initiation and departure rituals. Ask your frontline managers how they welcome and bring on new hires and how they bid farewell to people who are leaving the organization. One executive I worked with was horrified to learn that one team had an initiation ritual that bordered on hazing; it was quickly replaced with a new one.

Ask a friend to tour your offices. Ask this person to make note of symbols that support or contradict the flux principles you desire. Are there fancy corner offices and assigned parking spaces? Or are the hallways adorned with awards recognizing previously unsung heroes who went above and beyond?

Catalog your hero stories. What stories get told over and over again? In what contexts are they told, and what values do they reinforce? Also look into your company's vault to see what founder stories exist that aren't being told today and that you could potentially use to illustrate a flux principle.

Hire an anthropologist. Anthropologists are experts at identifying and understanding the lore of a culture. They know the questions to ask and the people to talk to, and they spend time immersing themselves to uncover hidden stories. More important, they have the benefit of looking at your culture with fresh eyes.

Once you feel you have a good understanding of what your lore is today, you can connect specific business problems or beliefs that you want to address with lore. Frame the problem or challenge as a question: How can a ritual create a stronger sense of agency? How can a symbol remind us of openness? How can a story lead to acting more quickly? Don't worry about getting it right: keep your options open, invite brainstorming, and give your new lore a trial to see if it sticks. Here are a few best practices to help you develop great lore that supports a disruptive culture:

Be disciplined about creating lore. To be effective, lore needs to happen with 100 percent reliability. If you start a new ritual, commit to doing it every time that it's expected. Don't be shy about repeating the same story over and over again. Be predictable, and continually connect the lore with a specific business need.

Schedule story time. Create space, no matter how small, for people to share their stories. When I was running Altimeter, I used to start staff meetings by inviting people to share how our company values played a role in their lives in the previous week. Sharing these stories gave us a glimpse into each other's world while also illustrating how we lived our values. Story time can be built into ceremonies of recognition and departures, staff meetings, and weekly communications. The key is to build it into the rhythm of your organization so that people regularly gather and share stories that are meaningful to them.

MOVING FORWARD

Take a step back and think about what you are trying to accomplish with your disruption operating model: keep your future customers close at hand, and hardwire that focus and intention directly into how work gets done in your organization. The closer you can get your team members to customers with your structure, process, and lore, the faster you will change and move to meet your future customers along their journey.

At times you may feel as if you are moving backward, slowing down to a crawl as you set up or rewire your flux culture operating system. Have patience! And know that the time and investment you make now will pay off handsomely in the future, epitomized by an organization that is resilient in the face of change and thrives with disruption rather than becoming weary by it.

TAKEAWAYS

- One of the biggest apparent contradictions of a disruptive transformation strategy is that you need the stable foundation of a cultural operating system to be the springboard for disruption. In a fast-changing world, people need to know what will *not* change in order to take outsized risks.
- Disruptive operating models consist of organizational structure, processes, and lore that are tuned to support the capabilities—openness, agency, and action—the organization needs to thrive in the face of disruption.
- Changing culture requires just one thing: that you do work differently. Be intentional in selecting what you do differently to build the new culture that you want.

CONCLUSION
· · · · · · · · · · · · ·

IN SEPTEMBER 2011, the former CEO of Google, Eric Schmidt, joined the new CEO, Larry Page, on stage at the company's Zeitgeist conference. Toward the end of the discussion, they were asked what the biggest threat to Google's continued success is. Page replied simply, "Google." Schmidt jumped in with an interesting insight: "Large companies are their own worst enemy, because, internally, they know what they should do, but they don't do it. Larry, what does he do all day? He's doing that. He's in there forcing the discussion, forcing the choice, and forcing the resolution that will ultimately determine how hugely successful Google is or not."

Both Page and Schmidt recognized that the gravitational pull of scale and incumbency applies to Google as well. They knew that the work of a disruptor is never done, that there is no easy path, and that it takes a determined, disruptive leader to force organizations to move forward.

The brutal reality is that most organizations that attempt a disruptive transformation will not succeed, and if they do, they won't stay disruptive for long. The few that do succeed realize that disruption, leadership, and culture are not a short-term solution to a problem; it becomes a way of life where you and your organization enjoy and thrive with it.

There is one company that began as a disruptive start-up and forty-eight years later keeps the three elements of disruptive transformation—a strategy inspired by future customers, leadership that creates a movement of disruptors, and culture that thrives with change at its core despite now being an industry leader: Southwest Airlines.[130]

HOW SOUTHWEST AIRLINES SUSTAINS ITS DISRUPTION MOJO

Southwest Airlines is famous for being a disruptor in the airline industry. Starting in 1971, the airline began flying between Dallas, Houston, and San Antonio in only one type of airplane (the Boeing 737) and using a point-to-point model rather than hub-and-spoke. Southwest kept its costs low by offering minimal perks and maximizing plane utilization with quick turnarounds at the airports. The company has followed this disruptive growth strategy since it was founded and has seen tremendous success. It has acquired three airlines, most recently AirTran in 2010, and expanded its operations to destinations in the Caribbean, Central America, Hawaii, and Mexico in recent years. Today Southwest Airlines carries the most domestic passengers of any other US airline while also having the fewest customer complaints as recorded by the US Department of Transportation.[131][132]

Even more astonishing is the fact that Southwest Airlines has been profitable for forty-six *consecutive* years in an industry notorious for volatility, mergers, and failures (see Figure 7.1).[133] That's not a misprint: forty-six years of continuous, consecutive operating profit from 1973 to 2018.[134] That profitable growth allows Southwest to push the envelope when it comes to exploring new avenues of growth, a disruption flywheel that is the envy of the airline industry. Southwest is continually disrupting itself. Changes that appear to be incremental or even routine at Southwest would be deemed highly disruptive initiatives at other airlines and companies.

Fig. 7.1 Operating Profit Margin for Southwest Airlines versus Worldwide Airlines, 1973-2018

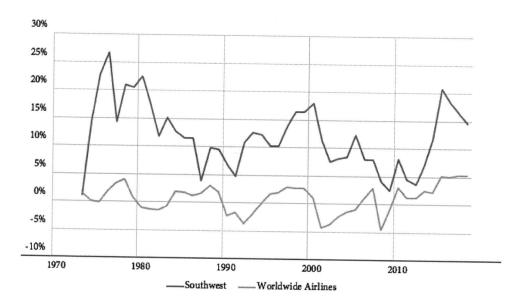

Source: IATA, ICAO, and Southwest Airlines

In an interview, Tom Nealon, Southwest Airlines president, credited the airline's success to the marriage of strategy and culture.[135] You can see this duality reflected in the company's values in Figure 7.2. The strategy reflects a complete commitment to be a friendly, low-cost airline. For example, Southwest Airlines allows two pieces of luggage to fly free, whereas other airlines charge for checked luggage. Every quarter, Wall Street analysts complain that the company is leaving money on the table, but executives steadfastly insist that changing that "bags fly free" policy would be anathema to the company's low-cost strategy. "We could bring in hundreds of millions of dollars in revenue by doing that," Nealon calculated. "I think it would be absolutely the worst thing we could do for the brand because that would be reneging on what we have promised."

Fig. 7.2 Southwest Airline's Values Reflect the Connection Between Culture and Strategy

Values			
Live the Southwest Way		**Work the Southwest Way**	
Warrior Spirit	• Strive to be the best • Display a sense of urgency • Never give up	Work Safely	• Follow standard operating procedures • Identify and report hazards • Respect and comply with regulations
Servant's Heart	• Follow The Golden Rule • Treat others with respect • Embrace our Southwest Family	Wow Our Customers	• Deliver world-class Hospitality • Create memorable connections • Be famous for friendly service
Fun-LUVing Attitude	• Be a passionate Team Player • Don't take yourself too seriously • Celebrate successes	Keep Costs Low	• Show up and work hard • Protect our ProfitSharing • Find a better way

Nealon recognized that it would be easy for the company to rest on past successes. "Being a disruptor in an organization that's been so successful for so long is a challenge," he explained. "Because why do you want to change it if it's working?" Southwest believes in challenging long-held assumptions because it's what its customers expect. When deciding what they will and will not change, they are guided by a north star. "There are a lot of things you might view as being really core to Southwest that we'll put on the table and talk about if we think we need to do it," Nealon shared. "But we won't challenge fundamental things around our culture and around what we expect of our leaders."

Anyone who has flown Southwest Airlines has experienced the quirky, maverick nature of its people and their spirit. "Many airlines have tried to copy Southwest's business model," Nealon observed. "But the thing that is much more organic and difficult to build and grow is the culture. We've been really protective of it and really thoughtful about sustaining our culture."

I've spent many days in the company's Dallas headquarters, and the walls of every hallway and conference room are covered with photos and memorabilia. The heritage of the company is literally around you in every corner of the building.

That culture permeates every aspect of the organization thanks to the Culture Committee created by Colleen Barrett, Southwest Airlines president emeritus, in 1990. Barrett made clear that the purpose of the committee wasn't to keep the culture the same, but rather to identify the best way to move the culture forward while still keeping its core tenets intact. Speaking a few years ago, she said: "One thing we should let go of is the sentence that, 'It's not the same old Southwest.' It's the Southwest that we make it. ...The old Southwest was the Southwest in '71, it was the Southwest in '81, and today it's the Southwest in 2015. And it's whatever we make it."[136]

At Southwest Airlines, culture creates a safe space for change to happen. Somehow, despite its success, it still feels like a scrappy company. "Even though we're the number one carrier in the United States and second largest in the world, I still see Southwest as the underdog," Nealon confided. He explained that the airline battles for customers city by city and that they are now moving into unchartered territory by expanding internationally.

For Nealon, culture is essential to the airline's growth and future. Recently, a team proposed a new way to board and deplane by using both the front and back doors. "That's a fairly controversial idea, and the team that came in and presented had to have a lot of courage," Nealon observed. He explained that Southwest Airlines was constantly conducting tests and learning experiments to challenge conventional wisdom. "Why would you want to challenge things like our brand platform or even open seating? The answer is because you can't sit still, you need to keep getting better. As long as we hear from customers that they want us to be thinking about things to change, we'll ask questions and figure out what is the right thing to do or not."

If you want your organization to sustain breakthrough growth for decades in the way that Southwest Airlines has, then settle in and get comfortable with disruptive transformation. This is the journey that you have chosen for yourself, a path that you were probably destined to be on. As a disruptor, you can't help but see the opportunities where others see only obstacles. It's your fate to want to change things for the better, to heed the call to step forward and be that lone nut crazy enough to believe that change is possible.

My hope is that this book has provided guidance for how to avoid being swept into the dustbin of disruption and to thrive with it instead. My hope is that you will find your fellow disruptors out there and that you'll draw strength and solace as you go on this journey. And my hope is that you will find success in creating the exponential change that our organizations, society, and world so desperately need.

ONE MORE THING
· · · · · · · · · · · · · · · · · · ·

When I began writing this book, I envisioned a day when leaders like you would have the resources and encouragement to lead disruption with confidence. I hope you've found the book helpful so far. But it's going to take more than a book to make a difference. It will take a movement, led by people like you who seek out and thrive with disruption to inspire and support our collective disruption efforts.

To help you and other disruptors, I have created Quantum Networks, a global network of disruptors who support each other to create exponential change and growth in their organizations, communities, and society. Being a disruptor can feel lonely, but it doesn't have to.

Imagine if we could find and connect with other disruptors, tapping into resources and best practices to drive our disruptive efforts further and faster—and to be there for each other as we aim high, stumble, and try again. Imagine the kind of change and impact we could create together.

Here's a partial list of what's available and under development at Quantum Networks, which includes a mix of paid and free public content:

Download a free eight-week guided program to develop a disruption mindset. Spend one hour a week, by yourself or with others in your organization, to systematically examine and change your strategy, leadership, and culture.

Subscribe to our weekly newsletter featuring best practices, case studies, and the latest news around creating disruption.

Engage in discussion groups to talk about topics ranging from tackling tough issues like strategy and culture to lighthearted inspiration to feed our disruptor souls.

Join a Quantum Circle, a small peer-based group that meets regularly to support disruptors on their journey.

In true disruptive fashion, I'm building Quantum on the fly. It's flawed, broken, and still learning how to walk. But my hope is that it will help you and other disruptors develop the courage and confidence to take the first step to lead change. Come see what we have cooking at quantum-networks.com.

Charlene Li

P.S. Can you do me a small favor? Once you finish this book, a review on Amazon is always deeply appreciated. It will take you a few minutes and would mean a great deal to me. Thank you!

ACKNOWLEDGMENTS

I like to make lists. But my problem with lists is that I lose them! As I sit down to write the acknowledgments of the many extraordinary and generous people who made this book possible, I know I'm going to forget someone. My apologies! Please know that you are in my heart if not on my list.

This book was three years in the making. Thanks to Mel Blake whose phrase "the disruptor's agenda" was the genesis for the book. Rohit Bhargava, my fellow author and the publishing team at Ideapress, helped me navigate the self-publishing landscape. (I had no idea that book pages aren't actually white.) Huge thanks to Genoveva Llosa, my patient and exacting editor who helped me figure out what I was really trying to say and do it with plain, straightforward language. Your wisdom and guidance turned my mash of words into eloquent relevance. Bev Miller sharpened the text with her copyediting to make the language flow for readers, and Briana Schweizer designed a book that draws people in with its elegance and simplicity.

Special thanks to Nathan Bjornberg who did the heavy lifting for the leadership analysis. His insights and advice guided the development of a powerful tool for understanding disruptive leadership. And a shout-out to my nephew Joshua Li for spending hours crawling through annual reports to gather the financial data for the case studies.

I'm grateful to the teams at Worthy Marketing Group and Smith Publicity for whipping my marketing and PR strategy into shape. From a new website to deep deliberations on the book's title and cover, their input was invaluable in shaping what you now hold in your hands.

This book wouldn't have been possible without the generosity of the people I interviewed for this book. Thank you for going deep, providing me with your insights, and sharing the most vulnerable moments of your disruption journey. And special thanks to the people who introduced me to those I interviewed: Megan Bourne, Michael Dunn, Jeff Goudji, Scott McAllister, Marten Mickos, Rüdiger Schicht, and Yaya Zhang. Their stories are here only because you made the connection between my book research and your network.

There's a special place in my heart for Kevin Eyres, Tony Fross, and Sarah Meier who endured early drafts filled with typos and nonsensical text to give me invaluable feedback and encouragement. Deep gratitude goes to Max Scheder-Bieschin who read the entire draft and provided feedback at a crucial time in the book's development. All of you provided much-needed perspective and encouragement that pulled me out of my writer's cave to see the light.

To Kim Harrison, Clay Hebert, Pete Longworth, Paul Pappas, and Josh Reynolds, thank you for the deep conversations about the book and pushing me out of my comfort zone. Honestly, my brain was buzzing and aching after talking with each of you.

For those of you who have ever tried to write while working full time, you know how important colleagues are in the process. Thank you to Prophet CEO Michael Dunn and senior partner Ted Moser for creating a supportive environment that allows me to be "Fearlessly Human" and bring my whole disruptive self to work every day. My thanks especially to Omar Akhtar, Leslie Candy, and Aubrey Littleton who helped me balance the research and consulting work at Altimeter with book research and writing. Your patient insistence on deadlines helped me get everything out the door. It wasn't always pretty, but it is always fun and fulfilling to get it done with you.

Saving the best for last, thank you to my partner in life and love, Côme Laguë, for your patience as I locked myself away for days on end, only to emerge to grab a quick dinner with you before disappearing again into the depths of my writing. I am so lucky to have married a man like you—someone who accepts me with all of my failures and flaws and always has faith that I can prevail even when my spirits are flagging. My deepest gratitude for your love and understanding.

APPENDIX
• • • • • • • • • •

"Apple: Think Different Manifesto," Ad Age, October 5, 2011

Here's to the crazy ones.
The misfits.
The rebels.
The troublemakers.
The round pegs in the square holes.

The ones who see things differently.

They're not fond of rules.
And they have no respect for the status quo.

You can quote them, disagree with them,
glorify or vilify them.
About the only thing you can't do is ignore them.

Because they change things.

They push the human race forward.

While some may see them as the crazy ones, we see genius.
Because the people who are crazy enough to think they can change the
world, are the ones who do.

© 1997 Apple Computer, Inc.

http://www.thecrazyones.it/spot-en.html We're not like other wireless companies.

The Un-carrier Manifesto, T-Mobile

We're not like other companies.

Why would we be? They're in the phone company business. We're in the changing the phone-company business.

We are unapologetically the un-carrier.

Unwilling to play by the rules they so fiercely protect. Unsatisfied with the status quo. Un-afraid to innovate.

And un-happy to be lumped in among them.

Some day when the history of the wireless industry is written, the chapter about today will be titled: What the Hell Were They Thinking?

This is an industry filled with long-term contracts, average penalties, termination fees, throttled data, no rewards for loyalty—everything that is the antithesis of what people love about mobility.

Consumers, today, live in the land of now.
Tweeting. Pinning. skyping. Posting. Streaming.

All in between texting and status updating.

This is the fertile, untapped territory where some company, our company, can ignite a sleeping industry. It's time to ask the same questions we hear wireless customers ask: Says who? Since when? And, what if?

"Wait a minute, I have to wait two years to get a new phone? Says who?"

"What do you mean my unlimited data isn't as unlimited as I thought? Since when?"

"Smartphones don't work in basements? Really? Well, what if...?"

We will ask these questions because we're thrilled to be working and tinkering and bringing the magic to what many have called the single most important device of our lifetime. A device that has changed the world—what insanity it would be not to change with it.

This is gigantic, magnificent stuff. Important stuff. And it's fun.

Becasue consumers don't need another AT&T. What consumers need is a company to stop acting like AT&T. They don't need another wireless carrier that's modeled itself after a utility company—they need a wireless carrier with a recognizable pulse that their customers can feel in the palm of their hand. A wireless company kept alive and nimble with the belief of being a better carrier, not simply another carrier.

We will give customers new phones right now instead of later. We will serve up all the data they need, when they need it. We will be the carrier to marry 4G to Wi-Fi for the most powerful nationwide service. And we will reward loyalty where other carriers don't.

This is all ours. More than a new carrier—a new category.

We are T-Mobile. The un-carrier.

And we will be un-relenting.

https://www.businessinsider.com/t-mobile-ceo-john-legere-un-carrier-manifesto-2016-10

Nextdoor, "Our Manifesto," Nextdoor.com, accessed April 6, 2019

We are for neighbors.

For neighborhood barbecues. For multi-family garage sales. For trick-or-treating.

We're for slowing down, children at play.

We're for sharing a common hedge and an awesome babysitter.

We're for neighborhood watch. Emergency response. And for just keeping an eye out for a lost cat.

We believe waving hello to the new neighbor says, "Welcome" better than any doormat.

We believe technology is a powerful tool for making neighborhoods stronger, safer places to call home.

We're all about online chats that lead to more clothesline chats.

We believe fences are sometimes necessary, but online privacy is always necessary.

We believe strong neighborhoods not only improve our property value, they improve each one of our lives.

We believe that amazing things can happen by just talking with the people next door.

We are Nextdoor. We are simply you and your neighbors, together.

https://nextdoor.com/manifesto/

(RED), "(RED) Manifesto," accessed April 6, 2019

Every two minutes a teenager is infected with hiv.

Yet it is preventable.

Aids is the leading cause of death among women worldwide.

Yet it is treatable.

Today 400 babies will be born with hiv.

Same thing tomorrow. And the next day.

Aids no longer has to be a death sentence. One pill a day. For just 30 cents can stop mothers from passing on the virus to their babies.

This is where you come in.

As consumers, we have tremendous power.

What you choose to buy, or not to buy, can impact someone else's life.

Every time you shop (red), share (red), dance (red), eat (red), a partner makes a donation to the fight against aids thanks to your choice.

Never before have our collective voices or

Our collective choices been so important.

There is an end to aids. It's you.

https://www.red.org/red-manifesto-1

Piedmont Health Manifesto

"At Piedmont Health, we are all in this for one reason-- to make a difference in every life that we touch. From our front lines to our back office and everywhere in between, we are all caregivers, working together behind the scenes to make you feel important and cared for. That means giving you our individual attention and using every resource, hu7man and digital, to seamlessly connect the dots across your healthcare journey. At Piedmont Healthcare, we have one priority: genuinely delivering genuinely good care. That's our way, The Piedmont Way."

NOTES

· · · · · · ·

Introduction

1   Michael Shapiro, "The Newspaper That Almost Seized the Future," *Columbia Journalism Review* (November–December 2011), https://archives.cjr.org/feature/the_newspaper_that_almost_seized_the_future.php.

2   David Folkenflik, "Knight Ridder Newspaper Chain Finds a Buyer," NPR, March 13, 2006, https://www.npr.org/templates/story/story.php?storyId=5259298.

3   Interview with Sverre Munke, former chief strategy officer and head of online classifieds at Schibsted, May 15, 2018.

4   *Schibsted Media Group 2018 Annual Report* (2019), http://hugin.info/131/R/2240156/883123.pdf.

5   A PwC study in 2017 measured the impact of disruption over a ten-year period from 2006 to 2015 and found that the rate of disruption was not increasing as measured by the annual shift in enterprise value of the top ten players in each industry. Paul Leinwand and Cesare Mainardi, "The Fear of Disruption Can Be More Damaging Than Actual Disruption," *Strategy Business,* September 27, 2017, https://www.strategy-business.com/article/The-Fear-of-Disruption-Can-Be-More-Damaging-than-Actual-Disruption.

6   Anna Washenko, "IFPI Global Report: Streaming Is the World's Top Music Revenue Source," *Rain News,* April 24, 2018, http://rainnews.com/ifpi-global-report-streaming-is-the-worlds-top-music-revenue-source/.

7   In their seminal book, *The Leadership Challenge, 6th Edition* (Hoboken, NJ: Wiley, 2017), coauthors Jim Kouzes and Barry Posner write, "The work of leaders is change. And all change requires that leaders actively seek ways to make things better, to grow, innovate, and improve."

8   My visit to the U.S.S. *Nimitz* almost didn't happen. I had harbored long-

simmering distrust of military action but I decided to move out of my comfort zone and go on the trip. I was impressed by the openness of the U.S.S. *Nimitz's* leaders who allowed sixteen bloggers to roam around the ship, sticking microphones and cameras into anyone we could talk to. And I'm grateful for the dedication of our military service members who spend months away from their loved ones to keep the world safe and provide humanitarian support in times of disaster. I learned to never judge a book by its cover and instead to always look inside it to discover hidden truths and treasure.

9   A special thanks and gratitude to my Altimeter founding partners, Jeremiah Owyang, Deb Schultz, and Ray Wang for having the faith to go all in with Altimeter.

Chapter 1

10 Google iterated early players like Excite! Lycos, Inktomi, and Yahoo! Facebook learned from Six Degrees, Friendster, and MySpace.

11 Clayton M. Christensen, *The Innovators Dilemma: When New Technologies Cause Great Firms to Fail* (Boston, Harvard Business Review Press, 2016).

12 "Major US Mobile Operators/Carriers Revenue 2011–2017," Statista., accessed April 4, 2019, https://www.statista.com/statistics/199796/wireless-operating-revenues-of-us-telecommunication-providers/.

13 "T-Mobile US Net Income 2005–2018," Statista, accessed April 4, 2019, https://www.statista.com/statistics/219463/net-income-of-t-mobile-usa/."Major US Mobile Operators/Carriers Revenue 2011–2017," Statista, accessed April 4, 2019, https://www.statista.com/statistics/199796/wireless-operating-revenues-of-us-telecommunication-providers/.

14 Jon Brodkin, "T-Mobile Takes $3 Billion AT&T Breakup Fee, Builds 4G-LTE Network," *Ars Technica*, February 23, 2012, https://arstechnica.com/gadgets/2012/02/t-mobile-takes-3-billion-att-breakup-fee-builds-4g-lte-network/.

15 Andrew Sherrard was the senior vice president of marketing at T-Mobile in 2012 and became chief marketing officer and chief operations officer in 2015. He left T-Mobile at the end of 2017. My interview with Sherrard was conducted on May 22, 2018.

16 One of the organizations that help with the process of understanding T-Mobile's customers and developing the strategy was my employer, Prophet. I was not part of Prophet when this work was done.

17 "Un-Carrier History/Un-Carrier Moves,", April 4, 2019, https://www.t-mobile.com/our-story/un-carrier-history. Interview with Andrew Sherrard, May 22, 2018.

18 Major US Mobile Operators/Carriers Revenue 2011–2017." "T-Mobile US Revenue by Quarter 2010-2018" Statista, accessed April 12, 2019. https://www.statista.com/statistics/219435/total-revenue-of-t-mobile-usa-by-quarter/.

19 Major US Mobile Operators/Carriers Revenue 2011–2017." "AT&T 2018 Annual Report", accessed April 12, 2019. https://investors.att.com/~/media/Files/A/ATT-IR/financial-reports/annual-reports/2018/complete-2018-annual-report.pdf. "Sprint 2018 Annual Report", accessed April 12, 2019. https://investors.sprint.com/financials/default.aspx. "Verizon 2018 Annual Report", accessed April 12, 2019. https://www.verizon.com/about/sites/default/files/2018-Verizon-Annual-Report.pdf

20 T-Mobile, "Mobile and Sprint to Combine, Accelerating 5G Innovation and Increasing Competition," August 13, 2018, https://www.t-mobile.com/news/5gforall.

21 Chris Gaither and Sallie Hofmeister, "News Corp to Acquire MySpace," *Los Angeles Times*, July 19, 2005, https://www.latimes.com/archives/la-xpm-2005-jul-19-fi-news19-story.html.

22 "Facebook Expansion Enables More People to Connect with Friends in a Trusted Environment," *Facebook Newsroom*, September 26, 2006, https://newsroom.fb.com/news/2006/09/facebook-expansion-enables-more-people-to-connect-with-friends-in-a-trusted-environment/.

23 Michael Arrington, "Facebook No Longer the Second Largest Social Network," *TechCrunch*, June 13, 2008, https://techcrunch.com/2008/06/12/facebook-no-longer-the-second-largest-social-network/.

24 Noemi Chaves, "Is MySpace Still Thriving?" *Jag Wire*, May 2, 2018, https://ohsjagwire.org/3255/2017-2018/is-myspace-still-thriving/.

25 "Facebook Users Worldwide 2018," Statista, accessed April 4, 2019, https://www.statista.com/statistics/264810/number-of-monthly-active-facebook-users-worldwide/.

26 Jillian D'Onfro, "Facebook Just Showed Us Its 10-Year Road Map in One Graphic," *Business Insider*, April 12, 2016, https://www.businessinsider.com/facebook-f8-ten-year-roadmap-2016-4.

27 You can find a full tool kit at https://www.ibm.com/design/thinking/. IBM has a very useful empathy map tool kit available at https://www.ibm.com/design/thinking/page/toolkit/activity/empathy-map.

28 "Empathy Map: Build Empathy for Your Users through a Conversation Informed by Your Team's Observations," *Enterprise Design Thinking*, September 28, 2017, https://www.ibm.com/design/thinking/page/toolkit/activity/empathy-map.

29 Jacob Sonenshine, "Netflix Has Doubled in Value This Year (NFLX)," *Business Insider*, June 14, 2018, https://markets.businessinsider.com/news/stocks/netflix-stock-price-doubled-for-year-2018-6-1027017550.

30 Michelle Castillo, "Reed Hastings' Story about the Founding of Netflix Has Changed Several Times," *CNBC*, May 24, 2018, https://www.cnbc.com/2017/05/23/netflix-ceo-reed-hastings-on-how-the-company-was-born.html.

31 David Becker, "Netflix Starts Streaming Service," *Wired*, June 5, 2017, https://www.wired.com/2007/01/netflix-starts-/.

32 Jason Gilbert, "Qwikster Goes Qwikly: A Look Back at a Netflix Mistake." *HuffPost*, December 7, 2017, https://www.huffpost.com/entry/qwikster-netflix-mistake_n_1003367.

33 Julianne Pepitone, "Netflix Hikes Prices for Plans with DVDs Streaming." *CNNMoney*, July 12, 2011, https://money.cnn.com/2011/07/12/technology/netflix_unlimited_dvd/index.htm.

34 Lisa Richwine, "Netflix Splits DVD and Streaming Services," Reuters. September 19, 2011, https://www.reuters.com/article/us-netflix-idUSTRE78I23B20110919.

35 Soo Youn, "People Were Not Stoked about Netflix Streaming When It Debuted," *Thrillist*, June 29, 2017, https://www.thrillist.com/entertainment/nation/netflix-history-streaming-in-2007.

36 Richard Brody, "Netflix and Qwikster: The Streaming Apology," *New Yorker*, June 20, 2017, https://www.newyorker.com/culture/richard-brody/netflix-and-qwikster-the-streaming-apology.

37 Ashley Rodriguez, "As Netflix Turns 20, Let's Revisit Its Biggest Blunder," *Quartz*, April 14, 2018, https://qz.com/1245107/as-netflix-turns-20-lets-revisit-its-biggest-blunder/.

38 James B. Stewart, "Netflix Chief Looks Back On Its Near-Death Spiral," *New York Times*, October 19, 2018, https://www.nytimes.com/2013/04/27/business/netflix-looks-back-on-its-near-death-spiral.html.

39 Rex Crum, "Netflix Surges as Sales, Subscribers Rise," *MarketWatch*, January 24, 2013, https://www.marketwatch.com/story/netflix-surges-late-as-sales-subscribers-rise-2013-01-23.

40 Mark Sweney, "Netflix Takes TV Gamble with $100m House of Cards Remake," *Guardian*, February 1, 2013, https://www.theguardian.com/media/2013/feb/01/netflix-tv-gamble-house-of-cards.

41 "Number of Netflix Subscribers 2018," Statista, accessed April 4, 2019, https://www.statista.com/statistics/250934/quarterly-number-of-netflix-streaming-subscribers-worldwide/.

Chapter 2

42 Interview with Mala Sharma, May 25, 2018.

43 Interview with Mark Garrett, April 19, 2018.

44 Interview with Mike Saviage, May 3, 2018.

45 Interview with Sharma. Jim Ludema and Amber. "How Adobe Enables Creativity Through Diversity, Psychological Safety and Values," *Forbes*, March 13, 2019, https://www.forbes.com/sites/amberjohnson-jimludema/2019/03/13/how-adobe-enables-creativity-through-diversity-psychological-safety-values/#727246987201.

46 Mark Bosworth, "The Upside to Being Let Go by Nokia," *BBC News*, January 31, 2014, https://www.bbc.com/news/magazine-25965140.

47 Siilasmaa shared that this enabled the management to focus their energies towards the business rather than fighting with their employees. An academic study of Nokia's Bridge Program found that 85 percent of the individuals laid off in Finland said that they were satisfied with the program. Both layoff candidates and employees who were unaffected by the layoffs remained productive—and employee engagement scores remained steady—throughout the restructuring. Moreover, there were no industrial actions in any of the 13 countries where layoffs happened. Sandra Sucher and Shalene Gupta. "A Better, Fairer Approach to Layoffs," *Harvard Business Review*, April 17, 2018, https://hbr.org/2018/05/layoffs-that-dont-break-your-company.

48 Jim Wilson, "Burn the Ships: Chapter One" (blog), Able Ebenezer Brewing Company, March 26, 2015, http://www.ableebenezer.com/blog/2015/3/26/burn-the-ships-chapter-one.

49 Christina Warren, "Adobe Goes All-In on Subscription Pricing Model," *Mashable*, May 6, 2013, https://mashable.com/2013/05/06/adobe-subscription-pricing-only/#.BEuC50TyPqf.

50 Frederic Lardinois, "Adobe Goes All-In with Subscription-Based Creative Cloud, Will Still Sell CS6 for Now But Will Stop Developing It," *TechCrunch*, May 6, 2013, https://techcrunch.com/2013/05/06/adobe-goes-all-in-with-subscription-based-creative-cloud-will-stop-selling-regular-cs-licenses-shrink-wrapped-boxes/.

51 "Sign the Petition," Change.org, accessed April 5, 2019, https://www.change.org/p/adobe-systems-incorporated-eliminate-the-mandatory-creative-cloud-subscription-model.

52 Chris Guillebeau, "Practical Ways to Burn the Ships: The Art of Non-Conformity," accessed April 5, 2019, https://chrisguillebeau.com/burn-the-ships/.

53 Interview with Paul LeBlanc, June 4, 2018.

54 According to the National Student Clearing Center's report, 22.1 percent of students enrolled in a private four-year, for-profit college graduated and 26.5 percent of those enrolled in a two-year institution. National Student Clearing

Center, "Completing College: A National View of Student Completion Rates –
Fall 2011 Cohort" December 2017, https://nscresearchcenter.org/wp-content/
uploads/SignatureReport14_Final.pdf

55 Chrystina Russell and Nina Weaver, "Higher Education and the Economic
Integration of Refugees," *Academically Speaking*, June 22, 2018, http://blogging.
snhu.edu/academics/2018/06/22/higher-education-and-the-economic-
integration-of-refugees/.

Chapter 3

56 Charles Rutheiser, *The Opportunity Makers* (San Francisco, Blurb Publishing,
2016).

57 Robert Kelley, "In Praise of Followers." *Harvard Business Review*, August 1,
2014, https://hbr.org/1988/11/in-praise-of-followers.

58 James M. Kouzes and Barry Z. Posner, *The Leadership Challenge: How to Make
Extraordinary Things Happen in Organizations* (Hoboken, NJ: Wiley, 2017).

59 Derek Sivers, "How to Start a Movement," TED, February 2010, https://www.
ted.com/talks/derek_sivers_how_to_start_a_movement.

60 "CES 2013 Day Two, Las Vegas—Highlights Video, Mobile World Live,"
YouTube, January 9, 2013, https://www.youtube.com/watch?v=L9d-H0tfHtE.
Start at 1 minutes 49 seconds.

61 "Martin Luther and the 95 Theses," History.com, October 29, 2009, https://
www.history.com/topics/reformation/martin-luther-and-the-95-theses.

62 "Karl Marx Publishes Communist Manifesto," History.com, February 9, 2010,
https://www.history.com/this-day-in-history/marx-publishes-manifesto.

63 Richard Feloni, "See the Manifesto T-Mobile's CEO Used to Take the
Company from Struggling to the Fastest-Growing Carrier in the US," *Business
Insider*, October 11, 2016, https://www.businessinsider.com/t-mobile-ceo-
john-legere-un-carrier-manifesto-2016-10.

64 Sharon Tanton, "How to Write a Business Manifesto," *Valuable Content*,
November 14, 2016, https://www.valuablecontent.co.uk/blog/how-to-write-a-
business-manifesto.

65 T-Mobile, "T-Mobile's Newly Named CEO Addresses Employees," YouTube,
September 19, 2012, https://www.youtube.com/watch?v=ZxwTJYVhIXg.

66 Feloni, "See the Manifesto T-Mobile's CEO Used."

67 David Goldman, "John Legere Credits His Sad Life for T-Mobile's Turnaround,"
CNNMoney, 2016, https://money.cnn.com/2016/03/28/technology/john-
legere-twitter-emoji-t-mobile/index.html.

68 Lucy Handley, "Meet John Legere, the Rule-Breaking T-Mobile CEO Who Loves Pink and Even Has His Own Emoji," CNBC, November 29, 2017, https://www.cnbc.com/2017/11/24/t-mobile-ceo-john-legere-on-twitter-his-rivals-and-being-an-uncarrier.html.

69 On April 6, 2019, John Legere (twitter.com/johnlegere) had 6.21 million followers. Verizon (twitter.com/Verizon) had 1.66 million followers, T-Mobile (twitter.com/tmobile) had 1.08 million, AT&T (twitter.com/att) had 869,000, and Sprint (twitter.com/sprint) had 429,000 followers, for a total of 4.1 million followers combined.

70 Drew FitzGerald, "T-Mobile's CEO Has a Side Hustle: Hosting a Goofy Online Cooking Show," Wall Street Journal, November 8, 2017, https://www.wsj.com/articles/this-goofy-online-cooking-show-host-has-a-side-gig-ceo-of-t-mobile-1510160040.

71 This exchange between Sprint CEO Marcelo Claure and T-Mobile CEO John Legere in 2015 is one example of how Legere interacted with the competition on Twitter. This is especially notable because T-Mobile is now in the process of buying Sprint. Twitter, July 23, 2015, https://twitter.com/marceloclaure tatus/624333609143521280?refsrc=twsrc^tfw|twcamp^tweetembed|twter-m^624335010087178241&ref_url=https://mashable.com/2018/04/30/sprint-tmobile-merger-ceo-twitter-beef/.

Chapter 4

72 This quote has been misattributed to Charles Darwin. It originated from a speech in 1963 by Louisiana State University business professor Leon C. Megginson. Over the years, it's been simplified in the retelling into a pithy quote. For more details, see "It Is Not the Strongest of the Species That Survives But the Most Adaptable," Quote Investigator, May 4, 2014, https://quoteinvestigator.com/2014/05/04/adapt/.

73 Interview with Max Hollein, June 14, 2018.

74 Robin Pogrebin and Jason Farago, "With Choice of New Director, the Met Gets a Scholar and a Showman," New York Times, April 18, 2018, https://www.nytimes.com/2018/04/18/arts/design/max-hollein-metropolitan-museum-of-art.html.

75 Ulrike Knöfel, "Frankfurt's Underground Landmark: Städel Museum Celebrates Bold New Extension," Spiegel Online, February 22, 2012, http://www.spiegel.de/international/germany/frankfurt-s-underground-landmark-staedel-museum-celebrates-bold-new-extension-a-816936.html.

76 "Political Correction Debate," Truthspeak, YouTube. May 18, 2018, https://www.youtube.com/watch?v=GxYimeaoea0&t=35m35s.

77 "Historic Attendance Records for Schirn, Städel, and Liebieghaus in 2012," Städel

Museum press release, January 9, 2013, http://newsroom.staedelmuseum.de/system/files_force/field/file/2014/trias_press_attendance_records_2012_logo.pdf.

78 Andrew Fox, "Building an Ancient City Block by Block: Teotihuacan in Minecraft," de Young Museum, October 26, 2017, https://deyoung.famsf.org/building-ancient-city-block-block-teotihuacan-minecraft.

79 "Contemporary Muslim Fashions," de Young Museum, February 4, 2019, https://deyoung.famsf.org/exhibitions/contemporary-muslim-fashions.

80 Emily Sharpe and José Da Silva, "Art's Most Popular: Here Are 2018's Most Visited Shows and Museums," *Art Newspaper*, March 27, 2019, https://www.theartnewspaper.com/analysis/fashion-provides-winning-formula.

81 Julia Halperin, "What Can New Yorkers Expect from the Met's New Director? Friends and Colleagues Call Max Hollein a Change Agent with an Artist's Touch," *Artnet News*, May 16, 2018, https://news.artnet.com/art-world/meet-mets-new-director-max-hollein-1286153.

82 Salvatore R. Maddi and Suzanne C. Kobasa, *The Hardy Executive: Health under Stress* (Homewood, IL: Dow Jones–Irwin, 1984).

83 For those of you familiar with my work from *Open Leadership*, some of the language may look familiar. That's because the underpinnings behind the model in that book and this one are similar, borne out by this research. In *Open Leadership*, the "optimist" and "pessimistic" mindsets are similar to the openness-to-change mindsets of disruptive leaders. The "collaborative" and "independent" mindsets are similar to leadership behaviors of disruptive leaders to empower and inspire. Charlene Li, *Open Leadership: How Social Technology Can Transform the Way You Lead* (San Francisco: Jossey-Bass, 2010).

84 To understand how disruptive leaders varied in their appetite for leading change, I asked leaders in my study to rate themselves on a scale of 1 (not disruptive at all) to 10 (extremely disruptive) on how disruptive they believed they are, with *disruption* defined as "challenging the status quo and trying to change a situation for the better." This produced a "disruptive quotient" score for each. The average reported disruption quotient score across all leaders was 6.1 with most of the scores falling between 4 and 8.

85 To arrive at these four archetypes, I asked the leaders how much they agreed—on a scale of 1 (strongly disagree) to 5 (strongly agree) —with a set of statements on leadership beliefs and also how often—on a scale of 1 (never) to 5 (almost always) —they engaged in a set of leadership behaviors. They were also asked to choose between a set of change mindsets which scaled from 1 (not comfortable with change at all) to 5 (highly comfortable with change). I compared their scores to determine whether they were above or below average when it came to these mindsets and behaviors. Finally, I analyzed how these

scores correlated with their reported disruptive quotient scores. For more details about the research, please visit charleneli.com/disruption-mindset.

86 For more information about the network of disruptors that I'm building, visit charleneli.com/quantum.

87 Melissa Korn, "Failure 101: Colleges Teach Students How to Cope with Setbacks," *Wall Street Journal*, December 18, 2018, https://www.wsj.com/articles/failure-101-colleges-teach-students-how-to-cope-with-setbacks-11545129000.

88 Li, *Open Leadership*.

89 *The New York* Times has an excellent article on "failure résumés" along with links to several examples. Tim Herrera, "Do You Keep a Failure Résumé? Here's Why You Should Start", *The New York Times*, February 3, 2019, https://www.nytimes.com/2019/02/03/smarter-living/failure-resume.html.

Chapter 5

90 This book details the early days of McKinsey's founding, especially the impact of Marvin Bower in establishing McKinsey's business principles. Duff McDonald, *The Firm: The Story of McKinsey and Its Secret Influence on American Business* (New York: Simon & Schuster, 2013).

91 Interview with Dominic Barton, June 13, 2018.

92 Paul Burkhardt, "McKinsey Apologizes for Overcharging South African Power Utility," Bloomberg.com. July 8, 2018. https://www.bloomberg.com/news/articles/2018-07-08/mckinsey-s-sneader-says-south-africa-s-eskom-was-overcharged. Walt Bogdanich, and Michael Forsythe, "How McKinsey Has Helped Raise the Stature of Authoritarian Governments," *New York Times*, December 15, 2018, https://www.nytimes.com/2018/12/15/world/asia/mckinsey-china-russia.html.

93 Charlene Li, *Open Leadership: How Social Technology Can Transform the Way You Lead* (San Francisco: Jossey-Bass, 2010).

94 The "open book" movement advocates for all company financial and performance data to be shared broadly with few filters except those needed to protect confidential salary information or legal proceedings. In some organizations, even salary information is shared to build trust that pay is fair and equitable.

95 Ray Dalio, *Principles: Life and Work* (New York: Simon & Schuster, 2017).

96 Risto Siilasmaa, *Transforming Nokia: The Power of Paranoid Optimism to Lead Through Colossal Change* (New York, McGraw Hill, 2018).

97 Before joining Nokia in 2010, CEO Steven Elop was an executive at Microsoft. In my interview with Siilasmaa, he explained that he led the negotiations with Microsoft to avoid potential concerns that Elop was influenced by Ballmer,

who was Elop's former boss.

98   Amazon's Leadership Principles are available at https://www.amazon.jobs/en/
     principles.

99   Jeff Bezos's 2016 shareholder letter is available at https://www.sec.gov/
     Archives/edgar/data/1018724/000119312517120198/d373368dex991.htm.

100 Interview with Paul LeBlanc, June 4, 2018.

Chapter 6

101 Manu Cornet, "Organizational Charts," Bonkers World. Accessed April 23,
     2019. http://bonkersworld.net/organizational-charts.

102 Satya Nadella, *Hit Refresh: The Quest to Rediscover Microsoft's Soul and
     Imagine a Better Future for Everyone* (New York: HarperBusiness, 2017).

103 "Satya Nadella Email to Employees: Embracing Our Future: Intelligent
     Cloud and Intelligent Edge," March 29, 2018, https://news.microsoft.
     com/2018/03/29/satya-nadella-email-to-employees-embracing-our-future-
     intelligent-cloud-and-intelligent-edge/.

104 "Definition of Lore in English by Oxford Dictionaries," *Oxford Dictionaries*,
     accessed April 7, 2019, https://en.oxforddictionaries.com/definition/lore.

105 DeAnne Aguirre, Varya Davidson, and Carolin Oelschlegel, "Closing the
     Culture Gap," *Strategy Business*, December 6, 2018, https://www.strategy-
     business.com/article/Closing-the-Culture-Gap.

106 Interview with Nick Jue, June 18, 2018. He is currently the CEO of ING in
     Germany.

107 William Kerr, Federica Gabrieli, and Emer Moloney, "Transformation at ING
     (A): Agile," *Harvard Business Review*, May 17, 2018, https://hbr.org/product/
     transformation-at-ing-a-agile/818077-PDF-ENG.

108 "Intermountain Healthcare Changing Internal Structure to Better Serve
     Patients and Communities," press release, Intermountainhealthcare.org,
     October 12, 1970, https://intermountainhealthcare.org/news/2017/10/
     intermountain-healthcare-changing-internal-structure-to-better-serve-
     patients-and-communities/.

109 Jeff Gregersen and Hal Dyer, "How Does Amazon Stay at Day One?" *Forbes*,
     August 8, 2017, https://www.forbes.com/sites/innovatorsdna/2017/08/08/how-
     does-amazon-stay-at-day-one/#d7146847e4da.

110 Huawei has its detractors and controversies, ranging from the arrest of its
     chief financial officer to the US government advocating that its allies not use
     Huawei's 5G equipment because of spyware concerns. I acknowledge these
     issues and decided to include Huawei in this book because there is much
     to learn from a company that has thrived with disruption and sustained

breakthrough growth over decades.

111 Sijia Jiang, "Huawei Expects 2018 Revenue to Rise 21 Percent Despite …, " Reuters, December 27, 2018, https://www.reuters.com/article/us-huawei-outlook/huawei-expects-2018-revenue-to-rise-21-percent-despite-international-scrutiny-idUSKCN1OQ0F9.

112 "China: Huawei Net Profit 2017," Statista, accessed April 7, 2019, https://www.statista.com/statistics/233043/net-profit-of-huawei/.

113 Interview with Joy Tan, April 9, 2018.

114 Interview with Omar Tawakol, December 18, 2018.

115 Interview with Sverre Munck, May 15, 2018.

116 Martijn Aurik, "How to Run a Meeting Like Google, Apple, Amazon, and Facebook," Minute, February 28, 2017, https://www.getminute.com/how-to-run-a-meeting-like-google-apple-amazon-and-facebook/.

117 Interview with Dan Liljenquist, July 17, 2018.

118 Lisa Eadicicco, "Here's Facebook's New Motto: 'Move Fast, with Stable Infra,'" Business Insider, April 30, 2014, https://www.businessinsider.com/heres-facebooks-new-motto-2014-4.

119 Amazon's Leadership Principles are available at https://www.amazon.jobs/en/principles. In his 2018 shareholder letter, CEO Jeff Bezos also explains the high standards principle in greater detail. "Amazon CEO Letter to Shareholders 2018," SEC, accessed April 7, 2019, https://www.sec.gov/Archives/edgar/data/1018724/000119312518121161/d456916dex991.htm.

120 Here's a video of the New Zealand and Tonga rugby teams performing their pregame rituals. I highly recommend full-screen, full-volume viewing. "Is This the Most Intense Haka EVER?" YouTube, November 13, 2017, https://www.youtube.com/watch?v=604o4vuEDoY.

121 Southwest Airlines CEO Gary Kelly has dressed up in costumes ranging from Paul McCartney of the Beatles, Captain Jack Sparrow, Dorothy from the Wizard of Oz, and Gene Simmons from the band KISS, complete with full face makeup. More at https://www.washingtonpost.com/news/on-leadership/wp/2014/10/31/the-outrageous-halloween-costumes-of-southwests-ceo/?noredirect=on&utm_term=.4bb76fd7fd01.

122 Interview with Tom Nealon, Southwest Airlines president, June 13, 2018.

123 Read more about this in Howard Schultz and Dori Jones Yang, Pour Your Heart into It (New York: Hyperion, 1997).

124 Learn more about LinkedIn's Bring In Your Parents program at https://bringinyourparents.linkedin.com/.

125 Jeff Stibel, "The Failure Wall," Dun & Bradstreet, April 16, 2018, https://www.dnb.com/perspectives/small-business/failure-wall-encouraging-culture-

success.html.

126 Pilar Guzman, "ONE Magazine: Handles with Care," *Smart Design*, https:// smartdesignworldwide.com/news/one-magazine-handles/.

127 "The Surprising Stories Behind the Peculiar Building Names at Amazon," *US Day One* (blog), November 21, 2018, https://blog.aboutamazon.com/amazon-campus/the-surprising-stories-behind-the-peculiar-building-names-at-amazon.

128 Disclosure: Electrolux is a client of my parent company, Prophet. A case study of the work done by Prophet for Electrolux is available at https://www.prophet.com/case-studies/electrolux-cx/.

129 "Burning platform" is a term developed by Daryl Conner, author of *Leading at the Edge of Chaos* and *Man gaging at the Speed of Light*, based on the story of an oil rig worker who leapt off a burning oil rig platform into the sea to avoid certain death. Conner uses it as an analogy to the courage leaders must have to jump into the uncertainty and ambiguity of change. Over time, the term has come to mean that change is only possible in catastrophic situations, which was not Conner's original intent. Learn more at this pos. "The Real Story of the Burning Platform", April 15, 2012, https://www.connerpartners.com/frameworks-and-processes/the-real-story-of-the-burning-platform.

Conclusion

130 Disclosure: Southwest Airlines has been a client of mine since 2013, and I have seen the company's leadership, operations, and culture from the inside out, warts and all. The company is far from perfect, but I come away from each engagement and encounter with deep respect for its commitment to its values, employees, and customers. And from my experience, pretty much everyone gives hugs instead of handshakes. It's just the Southwest way.

131 Bart Jansen, "A Record 965 Million People Flew Last Year, DOT Says," *USA Today*, March 22, 2018, https://www.usatoday.com/story/travel/flights/todayinthesky/2018/03/22/dot-record-965-million-passengers-took-domestic-foreign-flights-last-year/450679002/.

132 Department of Transportation, *Air Travel Consumer Report*, March 2019, table 6A , https://www.transportation.gov/sites/dot.gov/files/docs/resources/individuals/aviation-consumer-protection/335211/march-2019-atcr.pdf.

133 Airlines for America, *Annual Financial Results: World Airlines,* accessed April 7, 2019, http://airlines.org/dataset/annual-results-world-airlines/. The 2018 estimates are from "Industry Statistics", IATA, December 2018, accessed April 7, 2019, https://www.iata.org/publications/economics/Reports/Industry-Econ-Performance/Airline-Industry-Economic-Performance-December-18-Datatables.

134 Southwest Airlines, *Annual Reports*, accessed April 7, 2019, http://investors. southwest.com/financials/company-reports/annual-reports.

135 Interview with Tom Nealon, June 13, 2018.

136 "Southwest Airlines: Southwest's Own Colleen Barrett Talks Culture in 2015," May 6, 2015, https://www.facebook.com/SouthwestAir/videos/southwests-own-colleen-barrett-talks-culture-in-2015/10153422011443949/.

INDEX

ABOUT THE AUTHOR

For the past two decades, Charlene Li has had the fortune to be an author and analyst, exploring and explaining the new world and society being created right before our eyes by new technologies. In 2008, at the start of the recession, she founded Altimeter Group, which disrupted the industry analyst world dominated by players like Gartner, Forrester, and IDC, and which was acquired by Prophet in 2015. She continues to work with the amazing people at Prophet, helping create disruptive growth strategies for clients.

Charlene has authored many books including the New York Times bestseller Open Leadership and co-authored the critically acclaimed Groundswell. She appears regularly in media outlets such as 60 Minutes and the New York Times, and speaks all over the world. She is a graduate of Harvard College and Harvard Business School. You can learn more at charleneli.com.

That's what Charlene does. But what she lives, writes, and works for is creating the "A-ha Moment," that instance when people who are thinking through a perplexing problem are hit with recognition and understanding. A light moves across their eyes, followed by a smile. They go from being in a place of confusion--where something is happening to them--to a place of understanding--where they have agency over their situation. Helping leaders take that first step to empowerment and optimism, tempered by the knowledge of the journey ahead, is what drives her.